One Pot

One Pot

Love Food™ is an imprint of Parragon Books Ltd

Parragon
Queen Street House
4 Queen Street
Bath, BA1 1HE, UK

ISBN: 978-1-4054-9678-0

Printed in China

Photography by Mike Cooper
Home Economists: Sumi Glass and Lincoln Jefferson
Cover and internal design by Mark Cavanagh
Introduction by Linda Doeser

Notes for the reader
• This book uses imperial, metric, and U.S. cup measurements. Follow the same units of measurement throughout, do not mix imperial and metric.
• All spoon measurements are level: teaspoons are assumed to be 5 ml, and tablespoons are assumed to be 15 ml.
• Unless otherwise stated, milk is assumed to be whole and eggs are medium. The times given are an approximate guide only.
• Some recipes contain nuts. If you are allergic to nuts you should avoid using them and any products containing nuts. Recipes using raw or very lightly cooked eggs should be avoided by infants, the elderly, pregnant women, convalescents, and anyone suffering from an illness.

CONTENTS

Introduction

Mention one-pot cooking and most people will immediately think of stews and casseroles and these are, indeed, tasty, nutritious, and popular one-pot meals. However, there's far more to one-pot cooking—from stir-fries to pilafs and risottos, from curries to pot roasts, and from meal-in-a-bowl soups to gratins and roasts. The one pot you use is just as likely to be a wok or roasting pan as it is a pan or casserole. The obvious advantage to one-pot cooking is that there will be far less to wash and put away after the meal. This is no small consideration with today's busy lifestyle. As everyone tries to juggle the conflicting demands of work, family, and personal life, it's hard enough to find time to cook in the first place. However, you can also save precious time before eating, as well as after, by cooking in a single pot. Once you've done the preparation, many dishes can be left to simmer gently or bake in the oven while you get on with something else. Equally, others can be cooked in a matter of minutes in a wok or skillet. Also, lots of one-pot dishes freeze well, so if you cook double the quantity, which certainly won't take you twice the time, you can save a whole meal for another day.

When all the ingredients of a dish are cooked together, there's a uniquely delicious mingling of flavors and, just as important, all the goodness is retained in the cooking juices and not poured down the sink. Finally, one-pot cooking is good for the family budget and the environment as it uses less fuel.

The recipes in this book have been inspired by the traditional one-pot dishes that feature in the cuisines of almost every country in the world. Whatever the time of year and whatever your taste, you're sure to find something to please all the family. Take a culinary trip and choose from Hungarian goulash, Moroccan tagine, Spanish paella, Indian curry, Irish stew, French ragoût, Italian beans, Thai shrimp, and much more. Very occasionally, a recipe will require a supplementary dish or pan for part of the preparation, but as a rule, only one pot is required for the main cooking. Some of the recipes include an optional accompaniment of rice, noodles, or pasta, but if this seems like too much effort, why not try some of the delicious no-cook accompaniment suggestions on the following pages?

Accompaniments

Even one-pot dishes can benefit from accompaniments, but no one wants to undo all their good work by using more pans and dishes. Fortunately, there are lots of easy and quick options that can turn a meal into a feast.

Salads go well with a huge range of dishes and provide a contrasting texture, as well as extra vitamins and minerals. They take very little time to prepare, but for those who are just too rushed, most supermarkets offer a range of ready-made leafy salads, mixed salads, such as coleslaw, and bottled dressings. There's no excuse for salads to be boring, as the variety of salad greens available is vast. Add extra color with radicchio or red lettuce, spice up a plain salad with peppery arugula, and complement the flavor of the main dish with fresh herbs. Add crunch with radishes or croutons, a hint of sharpness with scallions or pickled beets, or refreshing coolness with cucumber and tomatoes.

Italians reckon that you cannot serve a meal without bread and they do have a good case with many one-pot dishes, especially soups, stews, and casseroles. Most supermarkets offer an extensive range of different breads, often baked on the premises. Baguettes and Italian breads, such as ciabatta and focaccia, are great for mopping up every last drop of the cooking juices. Naan bread serves the same purpose with Indian dishes and pita bread is the perfect partner for Greek and Middle Eastern meals. Tortilla wraps are just made for chili con carne. Garlic bread is always popular and is easy to make or can be bought ready-made. Similarly, croutons add that extra factor to soup.

Finally, don't overlook hot accompaniments that require hardly any effort to prepare. If you've got a casserole in the oven already, why not pop some potatoes around it to bake? Instant couscous just requires moistening with hot water—do check the label before buying. Soups are delicious served with a topping of thickly sliced French bread and grated cheese, flashed under the broiler. You can also add this to casseroles toward the end of the cooking time.

Essential Equipment

The most important piece of equipment for one-pot cooking is the pot itself—be it a casserole dish, skillet, saucepan, wok, or roasting pan. You will probably already have most of the other equipment you will require, such as knives, chopping boards, a slotted spoon or ladle, spatulas, a measuring cup, and oven mitts.

Flameproof casserole: This multipurpose pot can be used on the stove and in the oven. It can also be placed on the table for serving, especially if it is colorful or has an attractive design. Choose one with a heavy base to ensure even cooking. A cast-iron casserole would be your best buy, but remember that they are very heavy when full.

Saucepan: It is important to use the appropriate size for the dish otherwise the ingredients won't cook evenly, you may not have room to stir, or liquid can boil over. The most useful sizes for one-pot cooking are medium and large and the ideal material is stainless steel, which can be used on any type of stove. Make sure that they have tight-fitting lids.

Skillet: Choose a round, heavy-based skillet with a base diameter of 10 inches/25 cm. Sloping sides make it easy to slide a spatula in and out of the pan. If you prefer a nonstick finish, look for a hard-anodized lining which wears extremely well.

Wok: You can use a skillet for stir-fries but it is much easier to cook them in a wok because the slightly conical shape lets you keep the ingredients moving constantly from the sides to the center. A dome-shaped lid increases the versatility of a wok.

Roasting pan: Roasting pans are useful for cooking one-pot roasts. Make sure that the one you choose is large and solid, and that the sides are of an adequate height to prevent the cooking juices dripping over the rim.

Meal-in-a-Bowl Soups

Homemade soup is the ultimate comfort food and the perfect choice for a weekend lunch at any time of year. Serve it with crusty bread or rolls and, perhaps, some cheese and you'll have a filling, well-balanced meal for all the family. There are some very good quality bouillon powders and prepared stocks available nowadays, so it need not be a chore to rustle up a brimming bowl of soup, broth, or chowder.

Chunky Vegetable Soup

Put the carrots, onion, garlic, potatoes, celery, mushrooms, tomatoes, and stock into a large pan. Stir in the bay leaf and herbs. Bring to a boil, then reduce the heat, cover, and let simmer for 25 minutes.

Add the corn and cabbage and return to a boil. Reduce the heat, cover, and let simmer for 5 minutes, or until the vegetables are tender. Remove and discard the bay leaf. Season to taste with pepper.

Ladle into warmed bowls and serve at once with crusty bread rolls.

SERVES 6

2 carrots, sliced

1 onion, diced

1 garlic clove, crushed

12 oz/350 g new potatoes, diced

2 celery stalks, sliced

4 oz/115 g button mushrooms, quartered

14 oz/400 g canned chopped tomatoes in tomato juice

2$^{1}/_{2}$ cups vegetable stock

1 bay leaf

1 tsp dried mixed herbs or 1 tbsp chopped fresh mixed herbs

$^{1}/_{2}$ cup corn kernels, frozen or canned, drained

2 oz/55 g green cabbage, shredded

freshly ground black pepper

crusty whole wheat or white bread rolls, to serve

Minestrone

Heat the oil in a large pan. Add the garlic, onions, and prosciutto and cook over medium heat, stirring, for 3 minutes, until slightly softened. Add the red and orange bell peppers and the chopped tomatoes and cook for another 2 minutes, stirring. Stir in the stock, then add the celery, beans, cabbage, peas, and parsley. Season with salt and pepper. Bring to a boil, then lower the heat and simmer for 30 minutes.

Add the vermicelli to the pan. Cook for another 10–12 minutes, or according to the instructions on the package. Remove from the heat and ladle into serving bowls. Garnish with freshly grated Parmesan and serve with fresh crusty bread.

SERVES 4

2 tbsp olive oil

2 garlic cloves, chopped

2 red onions, chopped

$2^3/_4$ oz/75 g prosciutto, sliced

1 red bell pepper, seeded and
   chopped

1 orange bell pepper, seeded and
   chopped

14 oz/400 g canned chopped
   tomatoes

4 cups vegetable stock

1 celery stalk, trimmed and sliced

14 oz/400 g canned cranberry
   beans, drained

$3^1/_2$ oz/100 g green leafy cabbage,
   shredded

$2^3/_4$ oz/75 g frozen peas, thawed

1 tbsp chopped fresh parsley

salt and pepper

$2^3/_4$ oz/75 g dried vermicelli

freshly grated Parmesan cheese,
   to garnish

fresh crusty bread, to serve

Vegetable & Corn Chowder

Heat the oil in a large saucepan. Add the onion, bell pepper, garlic, and potato and sauté over a low heat, stirring frequently, for 2–3 minutes.

Stir in the flour and cook, stirring for 30 seconds. Gradually stir in the milk and stock.

Add the broccoli and corn. Bring the mixture to a boil, stirring constantly, then reduce the heat and simmer for about 20 minutes, or until all the vegetables are tender.

Stir in $1/2$ cup of the cheese until it melts.

Season and spoon the chowder into warmed bowls. Garnish with the remaining cheese and the cilantro and serve.

SERVES 4

1 tbsp vegetable oil

1 red onion, diced

1 red bell pepper, seeded and diced

3 garlic cloves, minced

1 large potato, diced

2 tbsp all-purpose flour

$2^{1}/_{2}$ cups milk

$1^{1}/_{4}$ cups vegetable stock

$1^{3}/_{4}$ oz/50 g broccoli florets

3 cups canned corn, drained

$^{3}/_{4}$ cup grated Cheddar cheese

salt and pepper

1 tbsp chopped cilantro, to garnish

French Onion Soup

Thinly slice the onions. Heat the olive oil in a large, heavy-bottom pan, then add the onions and cook, stirring occasionally, for 10 minutes, until they are just beginning to brown. Stir in the chopped garlic, sugar, and thyme, then reduce the heat and cook, stirring occasionally, for 30 minutes, or until the onions are golden brown.

Sprinkle in the flour and cook, stirring, for 1–2 minutes. Stir in the wine. Gradually stir in the stock and bring to a boil, skimming off any foam that rises to the surface, then reduce the heat and simmer for 45 minutes. Meanwhile, toast the bread on both sides under a preheated medium broiler. Rub the toast with the whole garlic clove.

Ladle the soup into 6 flameproof bowls set on a cookie sheet. Float a piece of toast in each bowl and divide the grated cheese among them. Place under a preheated medium-hot broiler for 2–3 minutes, or until the cheese has just melted. Garnish with thyme and serve.

SERVES 6

1 lb 8 oz/675 g onions

3 tbsp olive oil

4 garlic cloves, 3 chopped and
   1 peeled but kept whole

1 tsp sugar

2 tsp chopped fresh thyme

2 tbsp all-purpose flour

$^1/_2$ cup dry white wine

8 cups vegetable stock

6 slices French bread

3 cups grated Swiss cheese

fresh thyme sprigs, to garnish

Mushroom & Sherry Soup

Melt the butter in a large pan over low heat. Add the garlic and onions and cook, stirring, for 3 minutes, until slightly softened. Add the mushrooms and cook for another 5 minutes, stirring. Add the chopped parsley, pour in the stock, and season with salt and pepper. Bring to a boil, then reduce the heat, cover the pan, and simmer for 20 minutes.

Put the flour into a bowl, mix in enough milk to make a smooth paste, then stir it into the soup. Cook, stirring, for 5 minutes. Stir in the remaining milk and the sherry and cook for another 5 minutes. Remove from the heat and stir in the sour cream. Return the pan to the heat and warm gently.

Remove from the heat and ladle into serving bowls. Garnish with sour cream and chopped fresh parsley, and serve the soup with crusty rolls.

SERVES 4

4 tbsp butter

2 garlic cloves, chopped

3 onions, sliced

1 lb/450 g mixed white and cremini
   mushrooms, sliced

$3^1/2$ oz/100 g fresh cèpes or porcini
   mushrooms, sliced

3 tbsp chopped fresh parsley

generous 2 cups vegetable stock

salt and pepper

3 tbsp all-purpose flour

$^1/2$ cup milk

2 tbsp sherry

$^1/2$ cup sour cream, plus extra
   to garnish

chopped fresh parsley, to garnish

fresh crusty rolls, to serve

Borscht

Slice the onion into rings. Melt the butter in a large, heavy-bottom pan. Add the onion and cook over low heat, stirring occasionally, for 3–5 minutes, or until softened. Add the sticks of beet, carrot, celery, and chopped tomatoes and cook, stirring frequently, for 4–5 minutes.

Add the stock, vinegar, sugar, and 1 tablespoon of the snipped dill into the pan. Season to taste with salt and pepper. Bring to a boil, reduce the heat and simmer for 35–40 minutes, or until the vegetables are tender.

Stir in the cabbage, cover, and simmer for 10 minutes, then stir in the grated beet, with any juices, and cook for an additional 10 minutes. Ladle the borscht into warmed bowls. Garnish with sour cream and another tablespoon of snipped dill and serve with crusty bread.

SERVES 6

1 onion

$^1/_4$ cup butter

12 oz/350 g raw beets, cut into thin sticks, and 1 raw beet, grated

1 carrot, cut into thin sticks

3 celery stalks, thinly sliced

2 tomatoes, peeled, seeded, and chopped

6$^1/_4$ cups vegetable stock

1 tbsp white wine vinegar

1 tbsp sugar

2 tbsp snipped fresh dill

salt and pepper

4 oz/115 g white cabbage, shredded

$^2/_3$ cup sour cream, to garnish

crusty bread, to serve

Split Pea & Ham Soup

Rinse the peas under cold running water. Put in a large saucepan and cover generously with water. Bring to a boil and boil for 3 minutes, skimming off the foam from the surface. Drain the peas and wipe out the pan with paper towels.

Heat the oil in the saucepan over a medium heat. Add the onion and cook for 3–4 minutes, stirring occasionally, until just softened.

Add the carrot and celery and continue cooking for 2 minutes. Add the peas, pour over the stock and water and stir to combine.

Bring just to a boil and stir the ham into the soup. Add the thyme, marjoram, and bay leaf. Reduce the heat, cover and cook gently for 1–1½ hours until the ingredients are very soft. Remove the bay leaf.

Taste and adjust the seasoning. Ladle into warmed soup bowls and serve.

SERVES 4

1 lb 2 oz/500 g split green peas

1 tbsp olive oil

1 large onion, finely chopped

1 large carrot, finely chopped

1 celery stalk, finely chopped

4 cups chicken or vegetable stock

4 cups water

8 oz/225 g lean smoked ham, finely diced

$^{1}/_{4}$ tsp dried thyme

$^{1}/_{4}$ tsp dried marjoram

1 bay leaf

salt and pepper

Mexican-style Beef & Rice Soup

Heat half the oil in a large saucepan over a medium-high heat. Add the meat in one layer and cook until well browned, turning to color all sides. Using a slotted spoon, transfer the meat to a plate. Drain off the oil and wipe out the pan with paper towels.

Heat the remaining oil in the saucepan over a medium heat. Add the onion, cover and cook for about 3 minutes, stirring occasionally, until just softened. Add the green bell pepper, chile, garlic, and carrot, and continue cooking, covered, for 3 minutes.

Add the coriander, cumin, cinnamon, oregano, bay leaf, and orange rind. Stir in the tomatoes and stock, along with the beef and wine. Bring almost to a boil and when the mixture begins to bubble, reduce the heat to low. Cover and simmer gently, stirring occasionally, for about 1 hour until the meat is tender.

Stir in the rice, raisins, and chocolate, and continue cooking, stirring occasionally, for about 30 minutes until the rice is tender.

Ladle into warmed bowls and garnish with cilantro.

SERVES 4

3 tbsp olive oil

1 lb 2 oz/500 g boneless braising beef, cut into 1-inch/2.5-cm pieces

1 onion, finely chopped

1 green bell pepper, cored, seeded, and finely chopped

1 small fresh red chile, seeded and finely chopped

2 garlic cloves, finely chopped

1 carrot, finely chopped

$^1/_4$ tsp ground coriander

$^1/_4$ tsp ground cumin

$^1/_8$ tsp ground cinnamon

$^1/_4$ tsp dried oregano

1 bay leaf

grated rind of $^1/_2$ orange

14 oz/400 g can chopped tomatoes

5 cups beef stock

$^2/_3$ cup red wine

$^1/_4$ cup long-grain white rice

3 tbsp raisins

$^1/_2$ oz/15 g semisweet chocolate, melted

chopped fresh cilantro, to garnish

Spicy Lamb Soup with Chickpeas & Zucchini

Heat the oil in a large saucepan or cast-iron casserole over a medium-high heat. Add the lamb, in batches if necessary to avoid crowding the pan, and cook until evenly browned on all sides, adding a little more oil if needed. Remove the meat with a slotted spoon when browned.

Reduce the heat and add the onion and garlic to the pan. Cook, stirring frequently, for 1–2 minutes.

Add the water and return all the meat to the pan. Bring just to a boil and skim off any foam that rises to the surface. Reduce the heat and stir in the tomatoes, bay leaf, thyme, oregano, cinnamon, cumin, turmeric, and harissa. Simmer for about 1 hour, or until the meat is very tender. Discard the bay leaf.

Stir in the chickpeas, carrot, and potato and simmer for 15 minutes. Add the zucchini and peas and continue simmering for 15–20 minutes, or until all the vegetables are tender.

Adjust the seasoning, adding more harissa, if desired. Ladle the soup into warmed bowls and garnish with mint or cilantro.

SERVES 4–6

1–2 tbsp olive oil

1 lb/450 g lean boneless lamb, such as shoulder or neck fillet, trimmed of fat and cut into 1-inch/2.5-cm cubes

1 onion, finely chopped

2–3 garlic cloves, crushed

5 cups water

14 oz/400 g can chopped tomatoes in juice

1 bay leaf

$1/2$ tsp dried thyme

$1/2$ tsp dried oregano

$1/8$ tsp ground cinnamon

$1/2$ tsp ground cumin

$1/4$ tsp ground turmeric

1 tsp harissa, or more to taste

14 oz/400 g can chickpeas, rinsed and drained

1 carrot, diced

1 potato, diced

1 zucchini, quartered lengthwise and sliced

$3^{1}/2$ oz/100 g fresh or defrosted frozen green peas

sprigs of fresh mint or cilantro, to garnish

Hearty Winter Broth

Cut the meat into small pieces, removing as much fat as possible. Put into a large pan and cover with the water. Bring to a boil over medium heat and skim off any foam that forms.

Add the pearl barley, reduce the heat, and cook gently, covered, for 1 hour.

Add the prepared vegetables and season well with salt and pepper. Continue to cook for an additional hour. Remove from the heat and let cool slightly.

Remove the meat from the pan using a slotted spoon and strip the meat from the bones. Discard the bones and any fat or gristle. Put the meat back into the pan and let cool thoroughly, then cover and refrigerate overnight.

Scrape the solidified fat off the surface of the soup. Reheat, season to taste with salt and pepper, and serve piping hot, garnished with the parsley scattered over the top.

SERVES 6–8

1 lb 9 oz/700 g neck of lamb

$7^{1}/_{4}$ cups water

generous 1 cup pearl barley

2 onions, chopped

1 garlic clove, finely chopped

3 small turnips, cut into small dice

3 carrots, peeled and thinly sliced

2 celery stalks, sliced

2 leeks, sliced

salt and pepper

2 tbsp chopped fresh parsley,
   to garnish

Pork Chili Soup

Heat the oil in a large saucepan over a medium-high heat. Add the pork, season with salt and pepper, and cook until no longer pink, stirring frequently. Reduce the heat to medium and add the onion, celery, bell pepper, and garlic. Cover and continue cooking for 5 minutes, stirring occasionally, until the onion is softened.

Add the tomatoes, tomato paste, and stock. Add the coriander, cumin, oregano, and chili powder. Stir the ingredients in to combine well.

Bring just to a boil, reduce the heat to low, cover and simmer for 30–40 minutes until all the vegetables are very tender. Taste and adjust the seasoning, adding more chili powder if you like it hotter.

Ladle the chili into warmed bowls and sprinkle with cilantro or parsley. Pass the sour cream separately, or top each serving with a spoonful.

SERVES 4

2 tsp olive oil

1 lb 2 oz/500 g lean ground pork

salt and pepper

1 onion, finely chopped

1 celery stalk, finely chopped

1 red or green bell pepper, cored, seeded, and finely chopped

2–3 garlic cloves, finely chopped

14 oz/400 g can chopped tomatoes in juice

3 tbsp tomato paste

2 cups chicken or meat stock

$1/8$ tsp ground coriander

$1/8$ tsp ground cumin

$1/4$ tsp dried oregano

1 tsp mild chili powder, or to taste

chopped fresh cilantro or parsley, to garnish

sour cream, to serve

Bacon & Lentil Soup

Heat a large, heavy-bottom pan or flameproof casserole. Add the bacon and cook over medium heat, stirring, for 4–5 minutes, or until the fat runs. Add the chopped onion, carrots, celery, turnip, and potato and cook, stirring frequently, for 5 minutes.

Add the lentils and bouquet garni and pour in the water. Bring to a boil, reduce the heat, and simmer for 1 hour, or until the lentils are tender.

Remove and discard the bouquet garni and season the soup to taste with pepper, and with salt if necessary. Ladle into warmed soup bowls and serve.

SERVES 4

1 lb/450 g thick, rindless smoked
  bacon strips, diced

1 onion, chopped

2 carrots, sliced

2 celery stalks, chopped

1 turnip, chopped

1 large potato, chopped

generous 2^1/$_4$ cups Puy lentils

1 bouquet garni

4 cups water or chicken stock

salt and pepper

Chorizo & Red Kidney Bean Soup

Heat the oil in a large pan. Add the garlic and onions and cook over medium heat, stirring, for 3 minutes, until slightly softened. Add the bell pepper and cook for another 3 minutes, stirring. In a bowl, mix the cornstarch with enough stock to make a smooth paste and stir it into the pan. Cook, stirring, for 2 minutes. Stir in the remaining stock, then add the potatoes and season with salt and pepper. Bring to a boil, then lower the heat and simmer for 25 minutes, until the vegetables are tender.

Add the chorizo, zucchini, and kidney beans to the pan. Cook for 10 minutes, then stir in the cream and cook for another 5 minutes. Remove from the heat and ladle into serving bowls. Serve with slices of fresh crusty bread.

SERVES 4

2 tbsp olive oil

2 garlic cloves, chopped

2 red onions, chopped

1 red bell pepper, seeded and chopped

2 tbsp cornstarch

4 cups vegetable stock

1 lb/450 g potatoes, peeled, halved, and sliced

salt and pepper

$5^{1}/_{2}$ oz/150 g chorizo, sliced

2 zucchini, trimmed and sliced

7 oz/200 g canned red kidney beans, drained

$^{1}/_{2}$ cup heavy cream

slices of fresh crusty bread, to serve

Chicken & Leek Soup

Heat the oil in a large pan over medium heat, add the onions, carrots, and coarsely chopped leeks, and cook for 3–4 minutes until just golden brown.

Wipe the chicken inside and out and remove and discard any excess skin and fat.

Put the chicken into the pan with the cooked vegetables and add the bay leaves. Pour in enough cold water to just cover and season well with salt and pepper. Bring to a boil, then reduce the heat, cover, and simmer for 1–1$\frac{1}{2}$ hours. Skim off any foam that forms from time to time.

Remove the chicken from the stock, remove and discard the skin, then remove all the meat. Cut the meat into neat pieces.

Strain the stock through a colander, discard the vegetables and bay leaves, and return to the rinsed-out pan. Expect to have 4–5 cups of stock. If you have time, it is a good idea to let the stock cool so that the fat solidifies and can be removed. If not, blot the fat off the surface with paper towels.

Heat the stock to simmering point, add the sliced leeks and prunes to the pan, and heat for about 1 minute. Return the chicken to the pan and heat through. Serve immediately in warmed deep dishes, garnished with the parsley.

SERVES 6–8

2 tbsp vegetable or olive oil

2 onions, coarsely chopped

2 carrots, coarsely chopped

5 leeks, 2 coarsely chopped,
   3 thinly sliced

1 chicken, weighing 3 lb / 1.3 kg

2 bay leaves

salt and pepper

6 prunes, sliced

sprigs of fresh parsley, to garnish

Chicken-Noodle Soup

Put the chicken breasts and water in a pan over high heat and bring to a boil. Lower the heat to its lowest setting and let simmer, skimming the surface until no more foam rises. Add the onion, garlic, ginger, peppercorns, cloves, star anise, and a pinch of salt and continue to simmer for 20 minutes, or until the chicken is tender and cooked through. Meanwhile, grate the carrot along its length on the coarse side of a grater so you get long, thin strips.

Strain the chicken, reserving about 5 cups stock, but discarding any flavoring solids. (At this point you can let the stock cool and refrigerate overnight, so any fat solidifies and can be lifted off and discarded.) Return the stock to the rinsed-out pan with the carrot, celery, baby corn, and scallions and bring to a boil. Boil until the baby corn are almost tender, then add the noodles and continue boiling for 2 minutes.

Meanwhile, chop the chicken and add to the pan and continue cooking for about 1 minute longer until the chicken is reheated and the noodles are soft. Add seasoning to taste.

SERVES 4–6

2 skinless chicken breasts

8 cups water

1 onion, unpeeled, cut in half

1 large garlic clove, cut in half

^{1}/$_2$-inch/1-cm piece fresh gingerroot, peeled and sliced

4 black peppercorns, lightly crushed

4 cloves

2 star anise

salt and pepper

1 carrot, peeled

1 celery stalk, chopped

3^1/$_2$ oz/100 g baby corn, cut in half lengthwise and chopped

2 scallions, finely shredded

4 oz/115 g dried rice vermicelli noodles

Chicken Gumbo Soup

Heat the oil in a large heavy-based saucepan over a medium-low heat and stir in the flour. Cook for about 15 minutes, stirring occasionally, until the mixture is a rich golden brown.

Add the onion, green bell pepper, and celery and continue cooking for about 10 minutes until the onion softens.

Slowly pour in the stock and bring to a boil, stirring well and scraping the bottom of the pan to mix in the flour. Remove the pan from the heat.

Add the tomatoes and garlic. Stir in the okra and rice and season to taste with salt and pepper. Reduce the heat, cover and simmer for 20 minutes, or until the okra is tender.

Add the chicken and sausage and continue simmering for about 10 minutes. Taste and adjust the seasoning, if necessary, and ladle into warmed bowls to serve.

SERVES 4

2 tbsp olive oil

4 tbsp all-purpose flour

1 onion, finely chopped

1 small green bell pepper, cored, seeded, and finely chopped

1 celery stalk, finely chopped

5 cups chicken stock

14 oz/400 g canned chopped tomatoes in juice

3 garlic cloves, finely chopped or crushed

$4^{1}/_{2}$ oz/125 g okra, stems removed, cut into $^{1}/_{4}$-inch/5-mm thick slices

4 tbsp white rice

salt and pepper

7 oz/200 g cooked chicken, cubed

4 oz/115 g cooked garlic sausage, sliced or cubed

Turkey & Lentil Soup

Heat the oil in a large pan. Add the garlic and onion and cook over medium heat, stirring, for 3 minutes, until slightly softened. Add the mushrooms, bell pepper, and tomatoes, and cook for another 5 minutes, stirring. Pour in the stock and red wine, then add the cauliflower, carrot, and red lentils. Season with salt and pepper. Bring to a boil, then lower the heat and simmer for 25 minutes, until the vegetables are tender and cooked through.

Add the turkey and zucchini to the pan and cook for 10 minutes. Stir in the shredded basil and cook for another 5 minutes, then remove from the heat and ladle into serving bowls. Garnish with fresh basil leaves and serve with slices of fresh crusty bread.

SERVES 4

1 tbsp olive oil

1 garlic clove, chopped

1 large onion, chopped

7 oz/200 g button mushrooms, sliced

1 red bell pepper, seeded and chopped

6 tomatoes, skinned, seeded, and chopped

generous 4 cups chicken stock

$^2/_3$ cup red wine

3 oz/85 g cauliflower florets

1 carrot, peeled and chopped

1 cup red lentils

salt and pepper

12 oz/350 g cooked turkey meat, chopped

1 zucchini, trimmed and chopped

1 tbsp shredded fresh basil

fresh basil leaves, to garnish

thick slices of fresh crusty bread, to serve

Clam & Corn Chowder

Melt the butter in a large saucepan over a medium-low heat. Add the onion and carrot and cook for 3–4 minutes, stirring frequently, until the onion is softened. Stir in the flour and continue cooking for 2 minutes.

Slowly add about half the stock and stir well, scraping the bottom of the pan to mix in the flour. Pour in the remaining stock and the water and bring just to a boil, stirring.

Add the potatoes, corn, and milk and stir to combine. Reduce the heat and simmer gently, partially covered, for about 20 minutes, stirring occasionally, until all the vegetables are tender.

Chop the clams, if large. Stir in the clams and continue cooking for about 5 minutes until heated through. Taste and adjust the seasoning, if needed.

Ladle the soup into bowls and sprinkle with parsley.

SERVES 4

4 tsp butter

1 large onion, finely chopped

1 small carrot, finely diced

3 tbsp all-purpose flour

$1^{1}/_{4}$ cups fish stock

$^{3}/_{4}$ cup water

1 lb/450 g potatoes, diced

1 cup cooked or defrosted
   frozen corn

2 cups whole milk

10 oz/280 g canned clams, drained
   and rinsed

salt and pepper

chopped fresh parsley, to garnish

Laksa

Heat the oil in a large pan over medium heat, add the garlic, chiles, lemongrass, and ginger and cook for 5 minutes, stirring frequently. Add the stock and bring to a boil, then reduce the heat and let simmer for 5 minutes.

Stir in the shrimp, mushrooms, and carrot. If using the egg noodles, break into small lengths, add to the pan, and let simmer for an additional 5 minutes, or until the shrimp have turned pink and the noodles are tender.

Stir in the Thai fish sauce and cilantro and heat through for an additional minute before serving.

SERVES 4

1 tbsp corn oil

2–3 garlic cloves, cut into thin slivers

1–2 fresh red Thai chiles, seeded and sliced

2 lemongrass stalks, outer leaves removed, chopped

1-inch/2.5-cm piece fresh gingerroot, grated

5 cups fish or vegetable stock

12 oz/350 g large raw shrimp, shelled and deveined

4 oz/115 g shiitake mushrooms, sliced

1 large carrot, grated

2 oz/55 g dried egg noodles (optional)

1–2 tsp Thai fish sauce

1 tbsp chopped fresh cilantro

Bouillabaisse

Soak the mussels in lightly salted water for 10 minutes. Scrub the shells under cold running water and pull off any beards. Discard any with broken shells. Tap the remaining mussels and discard any that refuse to close. Put the rest into a large pan with a little water, bring to a boil, and cook over high heat for 4 minutes. Transfer the cooked mussels to a bowl, discarding any that remain closed, and reserve. Wipe out the pan with paper towels.

Heat the oil in the pan over medium heat. Add the garlic and onions and cook, stirring, for 3 minutes. Stir in the tomatoes, stock, wine, bay leaf, saffron, and herbs. Bring to a boil, reduce the heat, cover, and simmer for 30 minutes.

When the tomato mixture is cooked, rinse the fish, pat dry, and cut into chunks. Add to the pan and simmer for 5 minutes. Add the mussels, shrimp, and scallops, and season. Cook for 3 minutes, until the fish is cooked through.

Remove from the heat, discard the bay leaf, and ladle into serving bowls. Serve with fresh baguettes.

SERVES 4

7 oz/200 g live mussels

scant $1/2$ cup olive oil

3 garlic cloves, chopped

2 onions, chopped

2 tomatoes, seeded and chopped

generous $2^3/4$ cups fish stock

$1^3/4$ cups white wine

1 bay leaf

pinch of saffron threads

2 tbsp chopped fresh basil

2 tbsp chopped fresh parsley

9 oz/250 g snapper or monkfish fillets

9 oz/250 g haddock fillets, skinned

7 oz/200 g shrimp, peeled and deveined

$3^1/2$ oz/100 g scallops

salt and pepper

fresh baguettes, to serve

Meat Feasts

This chapter features slow-cooked, succulent stews and casseroles that simply melt deliciously in the mouth, whether beef, lamb, pork, or game. They have the additional benefit of being extremely economical because they use the less expensive cuts of meat. However, quicker-cooked but just as tasty dishes, such as a Chinese-style stir-fry and a Tex-Mex chili, are also included and it would, of course, be simply criminal to omit classic pot roasts.

Pot Roast with Potatoes & Dill

Preheat the oven to 275°F/140°C. Mix 2 tablespoons of the flour with the salt and pepper in a shallow dish. Dip the meat to coat. Heat the oil in a flameproof casserole and brown the meat all over. Transfer to a plate.

Add half the butter to the casserole and cook the onion, celery, carrots, dill seed, and thyme for 5 minutes. Return the meat and juices to the casserole.

Pour in the wine and enough stock to reach one-third of the way up the meat. Bring to a boil, cover, and cook in the oven for 3 hours, turning the meat every 30 minutes. After it has been cooking for 2 hours, add the potatoes and more stock if necessary.

When ready, transfer the meat and vegetables to a warmed serving dish. Strain the cooking liquid to remove any solids, then return the liquid to the casserole.

Mix the remaining butter and flour to a paste. Bring the cooking liquid to a boil. Whisk in small pieces of the flour and butter paste, whisking constantly until the sauce is smooth. Pour the sauce over the meat and vegetables. Sprinkle with the fresh dill to serve.

SERVES 6

2¹/₂ tbsp all-purpose flour

1 tsp salt

¹/₄ tsp pepper

1 rolled brisket joint, weighing
   3 lb 8 oz/1.6 kg

2 tbsp vegetable oil

2 tbsp butter

1 onion, finely chopped

2 celery stalks, diced

2 carrots, peeled and diced

1 tsp dill seed

1 tsp dried thyme or oregano

1¹/₂ cups red wine

²/₃–1 cup beef stock

4–5 potatoes, cut into large chunks
   and boiled until just tender

2 tbsp chopped fresh dill, to serve

Beef in Beer with Herb Dumplings

Preheat the oven to 325°F/160°C. Heat the oil in a flameproof casserole. Add the onions and carrots and cook over low heat, stirring occasionally, for 5 minutes, or until the onions are softened. Meanwhile, place the flour in a plastic bag and season with salt and pepper. Add the braising beef to the bag, tie the top, and shake well to coat. Do this in batches, if necessary.

Remove the vegetables from the casserole with a slotted spoon and reserve. Add the braising beef to the casserole, in batches, and cook, stirring frequently, until browned all over. Return all the meat and the onions and carrots to the casserole and sprinkle in any remaining seasoned flour. Pour in the stout and add the sugar, bay leaves, and thyme. Bring to a boil, cover, and transfer to the preheated oven to bake for 1¾ hours.

To make the herb dumplings, sift the flour and salt into a bowl. Stir in the suet and parsley and add enough of the water to make a soft dough. Shape into small balls between the palms of your hands. Add to the casserole and return to the oven for 30 minutes. Remove and discard the bay leaves and serve, sprinkled with parsley.

SERVES 6

stew

2 tbsp corn oil

2 large onions, thinly sliced

8 carrots, sliced

4 tbsp all-purpose flour

salt and pepper

2 lb 12 oz/1.25 kg braising beef, cut into cubes

generous 1³/₄ cups stout

2 tsp brown sugar

2 bay leaves

1 tbsp chopped fresh thyme

for the herb dumplings

generous ³/₄ cup self-rising flour

pinch of salt

¹/₂ cup shredded suet

2 tbsp chopped fresh parsley, plus extra to garnish

about 4 tbsp water

Rich Beef Stew

Combine the wine, brandy, vinegar, shallots, carrots, garlic, peppercorns, thyme, rosemary, parsley, and bay leaf and season to taste with salt. Add the beef, stirring to coat, then cover with plastic wrap and let marinate in the refrigerator for 8 hours, or overnight.

Preheat the oven to 300°F/150°C. Drain the beef, reserving the marinade, and pat dry on paper towels. Heat half the oil in a large, flameproof casserole. Add the beef cubes in batches and cook over medium heat, stirring, for 3–4 minutes, or until browned. Transfer the beef to a plate with a slotted spoon. Brown the remaining beef, adding more oil, if necessary.

Return all of the beef to the casserole and add the tomatoes and their juices, mushrooms, and orange rind. Strain the reserved marinade into the casserole. Bring to a boil, cover, and cook in the oven for 2½ hours.

Remove the casserole from the oven, add the prosciutto and olives, and return it to the oven to cook for an additional 30 minutes, or until the beef is very tender. Discard the orange rind and serve straight from the casserole, garnished with parsley.

SERVES 6

1½ cups dry white wine

2 tbsp brandy

1 tbsp white wine vinegar

4 shallots, sliced

4 carrots, sliced

1 garlic clove, finely chopped

6 black peppercorns

4 fresh thyme sprigs

1 fresh rosemary sprig

2 fresh parsley sprigs, plus extra
  to garnish

1 bay leaf

salt

1 lb 10 oz/750 g beef top round,
  cut into 1-inch/2.5-cm cubes

2 tbsp olive oil

1 lb 12 oz/800 g canned chopped
  tomatoes

8 oz/225 g portobello mushrooms,
  sliced

strip of finely pared orange rind

2 oz/55 g prosciutto, cut into strips

12 black olives

Beef Goulash

Heat the vegetable oil in a large pan and cook the onion and garlic for 3–4 minutes.

Cut the braising beef into chunks and cook over a high heat for 3 minutes until browned all over. Add the paprika and stir well, then add the chopped tomatoes, tomato paste, bell pepper, and mushrooms. Cook for 2 minutes, stirring frequently.

Pour in the beef stock. Bring to a boil, then reduce the heat. Cover and simmer for 1½–2 hours until the meat is tender.

Blend the cornstarch with the water, then add to the pan, stirring until thickened and smooth. Cook for 1 minute, then season with salt and pepper to taste.

Put the yogurt in a serving bowl and sprinkle with a little paprika.

Transfer the beef goulash to a warmed serving dish, garnish with chopped fresh parsley, and serve with rice and yogurt.

SERVES 4

2 tbsp vegetable oil

1 large onion, chopped

1 garlic clove, crushed

1 lb 10 oz/750 g lean braising beef

2 tbsp paprika

15 oz/425 g can chopped tomatoes

2 tbsp tomato paste

1 large red bell pepper, seeded and chopped

6 oz/175 g button mushrooms, sliced

2½ cups beef stock

1 tbsp cornstarch

1 tbsp water

salt and pepper

4 tbsp lowfat plain yogurt

paprika, for sprinkling

chopped fresh parsley, to garnish

freshly cooked long-grain and wild rice, to serve

Chili con Carne

Preheat the oven to 325°F/160°C. Using a sharp knife, cut the beef into ¾-inch/2-cm cubes. Heat the vegetable oil in a large flameproof casserole and cook the beef over medium heat until well sealed on all sides. Remove the beef from the casserole with a slotted spoon and set aside until required.

Add the onion and garlic to the casserole and cook until lightly browned; then stir in the flour and cook for 1–2 minutes.

Stir in the tomato juice and tomatoes and bring to a boil. Return the beef to the casserole and add the chili sauce, cumin, and salt and pepper to taste. Cover and cook in the preheated oven for 1½ hours, or until the beef is almost tender.

Stir in the kidney beans, oregano, and parsley, and adjust the seasoning to taste, if necessary. Cover the casserole and return to the oven for 45 minutes. Transfer to 4 large, warmed serving plates, garnish with sprigs of fresh herbs, and serve immediately with freshly cooked rice and tortillas.

SERVES 4

1 lb 10 oz/750 g lean braising beef

2 tbsp vegetable oil

1 large onion, sliced

2–4 garlic cloves, crushed

1 tbsp all-purpose flour

generous 1¾ cups tomato juice

14 oz/400 g canned tomatoes

1–2 tbsp sweet chili sauce

1 tsp ground cumin

salt and pepper

15 oz/425 g canned red kidney
    beans, drained and rinsed

½ tsp dried oregano

1–2 tbsp chopped fresh parsley

sprigs of fresh herbs, to garnish

to serve

freshly cooked rice

tortillas

Beef Stroganoff

Place the dried porcini mushrooms in a bowl and cover with hot water. Let soak for 20 minutes. Meanwhile, cut the beef against the grain into ¼-inch/5-mm thick slices, then into ½-inch/1-cm long strips, and reserve.

Drain the mushrooms, reserving the soaking liquid, and chop. Strain the soaking liquid through a fine-mesh strainer or coffee filter and reserve.

Heat half the oil in a large skillet. Add the shallots and cook over low heat, stirring occasionally, for 5 minutes, or until softened. Add the dried mushrooms, reserved soaking water, and whole cremini mushrooms and cook, stirring frequently, for 10 minutes, or until almost all of the liquid has evaporated, then transfer the mixture to a plate.

Heat the remaining oil in the skillet, add the beef and cook, stirring frequently, for 4 minutes, or until browned all over. You may need to do this in batches. Return the mushroom mixture to the skillet and season to taste with salt and pepper. Place the mustard and cream in a small bowl and stir to mix, then fold into the mixture. Heat through gently, then serve with freshly cooked pasta, garnished with chives.

SERVES 4

½ oz/15 g dried porcini
   mushrooms
12 oz/350 g beef tenderloin
2 tbsp olive oil
4 oz/115 g shallots, sliced
6 oz/175 g cremini mushrooms
salt and pepper
½ tsp Dijon mustard
5 tbsp heavy cream
freshly cooked pasta, to serve
fresh chives, to garnish

Beef & Vegetable Stew with Corn

Trim any fat or gristle from the beef and cut into 1-inch/2.5-cm chunks. Mix the flour and spices together. Toss the beef in the spiced flour until well coated.

Heat the oil in a large, heavy-bottom pan and cook the onion, garlic, and celery, stirring frequently, for 5 minutes, or until softened. Add the beef and cook over high heat, stirring frequently, for 3 minutes, or until browned on all sides and sealed.

Add the carrots, then remove from the heat. Gradually stir in the lager and stock, then return to the heat and bring to a boil, stirring. Reduce the heat, then cover and simmer, stirring occasionally, for 1¹/₂ hours.

Add the potatoes to the pan and simmer for an additional 15 minutes. Add the red bell pepper and corn cobs and simmer for 15 minutes, then add the tomatoes and peas and simmer for an additional 10 minutes, or until the beef and vegetables are tender. Season to taste with salt and pepper, then stir in the cilantro and serve.

SERVES 4

1 lb/450 g braising beef

1¹/₂ tbsp all-purpose flour

1 tsp hot paprika

1–1¹/₂ tsp chili powder

1 tsp ground ginger

2 tbsp olive oil

1 large onion, cut into chunks

3 garlic cloves, sliced

2 celery stalks, sliced

8 oz/225 g carrots, chopped

1¹/₄ cups lager

1¹/₄ cups beef stock

12 oz/350 g potatoes, chopped

1 red bell pepper, seeded and chopped

2 corn cobs, halved

4 oz/115 g tomatoes, cut into quarters

1 cup shelled fresh or frozen peas

salt and pepper

1 tbsp chopped fresh cilantro

Pepper Pot-style Stew

Trim any fat or gristle from the beef and cut into 1-inch/2.5-cm chunks. Toss the beef in the flour until well coated and reserve any remaining flour.

Heat the oil in a large, heavy-bottom pan and cook the onion, garlic, chile, and celery with the cloves and allspice, stirring frequently, for 5 minutes, or until softened. Add the beef and cook over high heat, stirring frequently, for 3 minutes, or until browned on all sides and sealed. Sprinkle in the reserved flour and cook, stirring constantly, for 2 minutes, then remove from the heat.

Add the hot pepper sauce and gradually stir in the stock, then return to the heat and bring to a boil, stirring. Reduce the heat, then cover and simmer, stirring occasionally, for $1\frac{1}{2}$ hours.

Add the squash and red bell pepper to the pan and simmer for an additional 15 minutes. Add the tomatoes and okra and simmer for an additional 15 minutes, or until the beef is tender. Serve with mixed wild and basmati rice.

SERVES 4

1 lb/450 g braising beef

$1\frac{1}{2}$ tbsp all-purpose flour

2 tbsp olive oil

1 red onion, chopped

3–4 garlic cloves, crushed

1 fresh green chile, seeded and chopped

3 celery stalks, sliced

4 whole cloves

1 tsp ground allspice

1–2 tsp hot pepper sauce, or to taste

$2\frac{1}{2}$ cups beef stock

8 oz/225 g seeded and peeled squash, such as acorn, cut into small chunks

1 large red bell pepper, seeded and chopped

4 tomatoes, coarsely chopped

4 oz/115 g okra, trimmed and halved

mixed wild and basmati rice, to serve

Beef Chop Suey

Combine all the marinade ingredients in a bowl and marinate the beef for at least 20 minutes. Blanch the broccoli in a large pan of boiling water for 30 seconds. Drain and set aside.

In a preheated wok or deep pan, heat 1 tablespoon of the oil and stir-fry the beef until the color has changed. Remove and set aside. Wipe out the wok or pan with paper towels.

In the clean wok or deep pan, heat the remaining oil and stir-fry the onion for 1 minute. Add the celery and broccoli and cook for 2 minutes. Add the snow peas, bamboo shoots, water chestnuts, and mushrooms and cook for 1 minute. Add the beef, then season with the oyster sauce and salt and serve.

SERVES 4

1 lb/450 g porterhouse steak, thinly sliced

1 head of broccoli, cut into small florets

2 tbsp vegetable or peanut oil

1 onion, thinly sliced

2 celery stalks, thinly sliced diagonally

2 cups snow peas, sliced in half lengthwise

$^1/_2$ cup fresh or canned bamboo shoots, rinsed and julienned (if using fresh shoots, boil in water first for 30 minutes)

8 water chestnuts, thinly sliced

4 cups thinly sliced button mushrooms

1 tbsp oyster sauce

1 tsp salt

for the marinade

1 tbsp Chinese rice wine

pinch of white pepper

pinch of salt

1 tbsp light soy sauce

$^1/_2$ tsp sesame oil

Osso Bucco

Heat the oil and butter in a large, heavy-bottom skillet. Add the onions and leek and cook over low heat, stirring occasionally, for 5 minutes, until softened.

Spread out the flour on a plate and season with salt and pepper. Toss the pieces of veal in the flour to coat, shaking off any excess. Add the veal to the skillet, increase the heat to high, and cook until browned on both sides.

Gradually stir in the wine and stock and bring just to a boil, stirring constantly. Reduce the heat, cover, and let simmer for $1^1/_4$ hours, or until the veal is very tender.

Meanwhile, make the gremolata by mixing the parsley, garlic, and lemon rind in a small bowl.

Transfer the veal to a warmed serving dish with a slotted spoon. Bring the sauce to a boil and cook, stirring occasionally, until thickened and reduced. Pour the sauce over the veal, sprinkle with the gremolata, and serve immediately.

SERVES 4

1 tbsp virgin olive oil

4 tbsp butter

2 onions, chopped

1 leek, sliced

3 tbsp all-purpose flour

salt and pepper

4 thick slices of veal shin
   (osso bucco)

$1^1/_4$ cups white wine

$1^1/_4$ cups veal or chicken stock

for the gremolata

2 tbsp chopped fresh parsley

1 garlic clove, finely chopped

grated rind of 1 lemon

Braised Veal in Red Wine

Preheat the oven to 350°F/180°C. Put the flour and pepper to taste in a plastic bag, add the meat, and shake well to coat each piece. Heat the oil in a large, ovenproof casserole. Add the meat, in batches, and cook for 5–10 minutes, stirring constantly, until browned all over. Remove with a slotted spoon and set aside.

Add the whole onions, garlic, and carrots to the casserole and cook, stirring frequently, for 5 minutes until beginning to soften. Return the meat to the casserole. Pour in the wine, scraping any sediment from the bottom of the casserole, then add the stock, tomatoes with their juice, lemon rind, bay leaf, parsley, basil, thyme, and salt and pepper to taste. Bring to a boil, then cover the casserole.

Transfer to the preheated oven and cook for 2 hours, or until the meat is tender.

Serve hot, garnished with extra chopped parsley and accompanied by freshly cooked rice.

SERVES 6

scant $1/4$ cup all-purpose flour

salt and pepper

2 lb/900 g braising veal or beef, cubed

4 tbsp olive oil

12 oz/350 g white onions

2 garlic cloves, finely chopped

12 oz/350 g carrots, sliced

$1 1/4$ cups full-bodied red wine

$2/3$ cup beef or chicken stock

14 oz/400 g canned chopped tomatoes with herbs in juice

pared rind of 1 lemon

1 bay leaf

1 tbsp chopped fresh flat-leaf parsley, plus extra to garnish

1 tbsp chopped fresh basil

1 tsp chopped fresh thyme

freshly cooked rice, to serve

Roast Lamb with Orzo

Preheat the oven to 350°F/180°C. Untie the lamb and open out. Arrange the lemon slices down the center and sprinkle over half the oregano, the chopped garlic, and salt and pepper to taste. Roll up the meat and tie with string. Cut slits all over the lamb and insert a garlic slice into each slit.

Put the tomatoes with their juice, cold water, remaining oregano, the sugar, and bay leaf in a large roasting pan. Put the lamb on top, drizzle over the oil, and season to taste with salt and pepper.

Roast the lamb in the preheated oven for 1 hour 5 minutes. 15 minutes before the end of the cooking time, stir the boiling water and orzo into the tomatoes in the pan. Add a little extra water if the sauce seems too thick. Return to the oven for an additional 15 minutes, or until the lamb and orzo are tender and the tomatoes are reduced to a thick sauce.

To serve, carve the lamb into slices and serve hot with the orzo and tomato sauce.

SERVES 4

1 boned leg or shoulder of lamb, weighing 1 lb 10 oz/750 g

$1/2$ lemon, thinly sliced

1 tbsp chopped fresh oregano

4 large garlic cloves, 2 finely chopped and 2 thinly sliced

salt and pepper

1 lb 12 oz/800 g canned chopped tomatoes in juice

$2/3$ cup cold water

pinch of sugar

1 bay leaf

2 tbsp olive oil

$2/3$ cup boiling water

generous 1 cup dried orzo or short-grain rice

Lamb Shanks

Dry-roast the coriander and cumin seeds until fragrant, then pound with the cinnamon, chile, and 2 garlic cloves in a mortar with a pestle. Stir in half the oil and the lime rind. Rub the spice paste all over the lamb and marinate for 4 hours.

Preheat the oven to 400°F/200°C. Heat the remaining oil in a flameproof casserole and cook the lamb, turning frequently, until evenly browned. Chop the remaining garlic and add to the casserole with the onions, carrots, celery, and lime, then pour in enough stock or water to cover. Stir in the tomato paste, add the herbs, and season with salt and pepper.

Cover and cook in the preheated oven for 30 minutes. Reduce the oven temperature to 325°F/160°C and cook for an additional 3 hours, or until very tender.

Transfer the lamb to a dish. Strain the cooking liquid to remove any solids, then return the liquid to the casserole. Boil until reduced and thickened. Serve the lamb with the sauce poured over it, garnished with sprigs of rosemary.

SERVES 6

1 tsp coriander seeds

1 tsp cumin seeds

1 tsp ground cinnamon

1 fresh green chile, seeded and finely chopped

1 garlic bulb, separated into cloves

$^{1}/_{2}$ cup peanut or sunflower oil

grated rind of 1 lime

6 lamb shanks

2 onions, chopped

2 carrots, chopped

2 celery stalks, chopped

1 lime, chopped

3 cups beef stock or water

1 tsp sun-dried tomato paste

2 fresh mint sprigs

2 fresh rosemary sprigs, plus extra to garnish

salt and pepper

Lamb & Potato Stew

Preheat the oven to 325°F/160°C. Spread the flour on a plate and season with salt and pepper. Roll the pieces of lamb in the flour to coat, shaking off any excess, and arrange in the bottom of a casserole.

Layer the onions, carrots, and potatoes on top of the lamb.

Sprinkle in the thyme and pour in the stock, then cover and cook in the preheated oven for 2$\frac{1}{2}$ hours. Garnish with the chopped parsley and serve straight from the casserole.

SERVES 4

4 tbsp all-purpose flour

salt and pepper

3 lb/1.3 kg middle neck of lamb, trimmed of visible fat

3 large onions, chopped

3 carrots, sliced

1 lb/450 g potatoes, cut into quarters

$\frac{1}{2}$ tsp dried thyme

scant 3$\frac{1}{2}$ cups hot beef stock

2 tbsp chopped fresh parsley, to garnish

Lamb Stew with Chickpeas

Heat 4 tablespoons of the oil in a large, heavy-bottom flameproof casserole over medium-high heat. Reduce the heat, add the chorizo, and cook for 1 minute. Transfer to a plate. Add the onions to the casserole and cook for 2 minutes, then add the garlic and continue cooking for 3 minutes, or until the onions are soft, but not brown. Remove from the casserole and set aside.

Heat the remaining 2 tablespoons of oil in the casserole. Add the lamb cubes in a single layer without overcrowding the casserole, and cook until browned on each side; work in batches, if necessary.

Return the onion mixture and chorizo to the casserole with all the lamb. Stir in the stock, wine, vinegar, tomatoes with their juices, and salt and pepper to taste. Bring to a boil, scraping any glazed bits from the bottom of the casserole. Reduce the heat and stir in the thyme, bay leaves, and paprika.

Transfer to a preheated oven, 325°F/160°C, and cook, covered, for 40–45 minutes until the lamb is tender. Stir in the chickpeas and return to the oven, uncovered, for 10 minutes, or until they are heated through and the juices are reduced.

Taste and adjust the seasoning. Garnish with thyme and serve.

SERVES 4–6

6 tbsp olive oil

8 oz/225 g chorizo sausage, cut into $^1/_4$-inch/5-mm thick slices, casings removed

2 large onions, chopped

6 large garlic cloves, crushed

2 lb/900 g boned leg of lamb, cut into 2-inch/5-cm chunks

scant 1$^1/_4$ cups lamb stock or water

$^1/_2$ cup red wine, such as Rioja or Tempranillo

2 tbsp sherry vinegar

1 lb 12 oz/800 g canned chopped tomatoes

salt and pepper

4 sprigs fresh thyme

2 bay leaves

$^1/_2$ tsp sweet Spanish paprika

1 lb 12 oz/800 g canned chickpeas, rinsed and drained

sprigs of fresh thyme, to garnish

Mediterranean Lamb with Apricots & Pistachios

Put the saffron threads in a heatproof pitcher with the water and let stand for at least 10 minutes to infuse. Trim off any fat or gristle from the lamb and cut into 1-inch/2.5-cm chunks. Mix the flour and spices together, then toss the lamb in the spiced flour until well coated and reserve any remaining spiced flour.

Heat the oil in a large, heavy-bottom pan and cook the onion and garlic, stirring frequently, for 5 minutes, or until softened. Add the lamb and cook over high heat, stirring frequently, for 3 minutes, or until browned on all sides and sealed. Sprinkle in the reserved spiced flour and cook, stirring constantly, for 2 minutes, then remove from the heat.

Gradually stir in the stock and the saffron and its soaking liquid, then return to the heat and bring to a boil, stirring. Add the cinnamon stick and apricots. Reduce the heat, then cover and simmer, stirring occasionally, for 1 hour.

Add the zucchini and tomatoes and cook for an additional 15 minutes. Discard the cinnamon stick. Stir in the fresh cilantro and season to taste with salt and pepper. Serve sprinkled with the pistachios, accompanied by couscous.

SERVES 4

pinch of saffron threads

2 tbsp almost boiling water

1 lb/450 g lean boneless lamb, such as leg steaks

$1^1/_2$ tbsp all-purpose flour

1 tsp ground coriander

$^1/_2$ tsp ground cumin

$^1/_2$ tsp ground allspice

1 tbsp olive oil

1 onion, chopped

2–3 garlic cloves, chopped

scant 2 cups lamb or chicken stock

1 cinnamon stick, bruised

$^1/_2$ cup dried apricots, coarsely chopped

6 oz/175 g zucchini, sliced into half moons

4 oz/115 g cherry tomatoes

1 tbsp chopped fresh cilantro

salt and pepper

2 tbsp coarsely chopped pistachios, to garnish

couscous, to serve

Cinnamon Lamb Casserole

Season the flour with salt and pepper to taste and put it with the lamb in a plastic bag, then hold the top closed and shake until the lamb cubes are lightly coated all over. Remove the lamb from the bag, then shake off any excess flour and set aside.

Heat the oil in a large, flameproof casserole and cook the onions and garlic, stirring frequently, for 5 minutes, or until softened. Add the lamb and cook over high heat, stirring frequently, for 5 minutes, or until browned on all sides and sealed.

Stir the wine, vinegar, and tomatoes and their juice into the casserole, scraping any sediment from the bottom of the casserole, and bring to a boil. Reduce the heat and add the raisins, cinnamon, sugar, and bay leaf. Season to taste with salt and pepper. Cover and simmer gently for 2 hours, or until the lamb is tender.

Meanwhile, make the topping. Put the yogurt into a small serving bowl, then stir in the garlic and season to taste with salt and pepper. Cover and chill in the refrigerator until required.

Discard the bay leaf and serve the lamb hot, topped with a spoonful of the garlic yogurt and dusted with paprika.

SERVES 6

2 tbsp all-purpose flour

salt and pepper

2 lb 4 oz/1 kg lean boneless lamb, cubed

2 tbsp olive oil

2 large onions, sliced

1 garlic clove, finely chopped

$1^1/_4$ cups full-bodied red wine

2 tbsp red wine vinegar

14 oz/400 g canned chopped tomatoes

generous $^1/_3$ cup seedless raisins

1 tbsp ground cinnamon

pinch of sugar

1 bay leaf

paprika, to garnish

for the topping

$^2/_3$ cup plain yogurt

2 garlic cloves, crushed

salt and pepper

Country Lamb Casserole

Preheat the oven to 350°F/180°C. Heat the oil in a large, flameproof casserole. Add the lamb in batches and cook over medium heat, stirring, for 5–8 minutes, or until browned. Transfer to a plate.

Add the sliced leeks to the casserole and cook, stirring occasionally, for 5 minutes, or until softened. Sprinkle in the flour and cook, stirring, for 1 minute. Pour in the wine and stock and bring to a boil, stirring. Stir in the tomato paste, sugar, chopped mint, and apricots and season to taste with salt and pepper.

Return the lamb to the casserole and stir. Arrange the potato slices on top and brush with the melted butter. Cover and bake in the preheated oven for 1½ hours.

Increase the oven temperature to 400°F/200°C, uncover the casserole, and bake for an additional 30 minutes, or until the potato topping is golden brown. Serve immediately, garnished with fresh mint sprigs.

SERVES 6

2 tbsp corn oil

4 lb 8 oz/2 kg boneless leg of lamb, cut into 1-inch/2.5-cm cubes

6 leeks, sliced

1 tbsp all-purpose flour

$2/3$ cup rosé wine

$1^1/4$ cups chicken stock

1 tbsp tomato paste

1 tbsp sugar

2 tbsp chopped fresh mint

4 oz/115 g dried apricots, chopped

salt and pepper

2 lb 4 oz/1 kg potatoes, sliced

3 tbsp melted unsalted butter

fresh mint sprigs, to garnish

Lamb with Pears

Preheat the oven to 325°F/160°C. Heat the olive oil in a flameproof casserole over medium heat. Add the lamb and cook, turning frequently, for 5–10 minutes, or until browned on all sides.

Arrange the pear pieces on top, then sprinkle over the ginger. Cover with the potatoes. Pour in the cider and season to taste with salt and pepper. Cover and cook in the preheated oven for 1¹/₄ hours.

Trim the stem ends of the green beans. Remove the casserole from the oven and add the beans, then re-cover and return to the oven for an additional 30 minutes. Taste and adjust the seasoning and sprinkle with the chives. Serve immediately.

SERVES 4

1 tbsp olive oil

2 lb 4 oz/1 kg best end-of-neck lamb cutlets, trimmed of visible fat

6 pears, peeled, cored, and cut into quarters

1 tsp ground ginger

4 potatoes, diced

4 tbsp hard cider

salt and pepper

1 lb/450 g green beans

2 tbsp snipped fresh chives, to garnish

Azerbaijani Lamb Pilaf

Heat the oil in a large flameproof casserole or pan over high heat. Add the lamb, in batches, and cook over high heat, turning frequently, for 7 minutes, or until lightly browned.

Add the onions, reduce the heat to medium, and cook for 2 minutes, or until beginning to soften. Add the cumin and rice and cook, stirring to coat, for 2 minutes, or until the rice is translucent. Stir in the tomato paste and the saffron threads.

Add the pomegranate juice and stock. Bring to a boil, stirring. Stir in the apricots and raisins. Reduce the heat to low, cover, and simmer for 20–25 minutes, or until the lamb and rice are tender and all of the liquid has been absorbed.

Season to taste with salt and pepper, then sprinkle the shredded mint and watercress over the pilaf and serve straight from the casserole.

SERVES 4

2–3 tbsp vegetable oil

1 lb 7 oz/650 g boneless lamb shoulder, cut into 1-inch/2.5-cm cubes

2 onions, coarsely chopped

1 tsp ground cumin

7 oz/200 g risotto rice

1 tbsp tomato paste

1 tsp saffron threads

scant ½ cup pomegranate juice

scant 3½ cups lamb stock, chicken stock, or water

4 oz/115 g dried apricots or prunes, halved

2 tbsp raisins

salt and pepper

2 tbsp shredded fresh mint

2 tbsp shredded fresh watercress or arugula

Pot-roast Pork

Heat the oil with half the butter in a heavy-bottom pan or flameproof casserole. Add the pork and cook over medium heat, turning frequently, for 5–10 minutes, or until browned. Transfer to a plate.

Add the shallots to the pan and cook, stirring frequently, for 5 minutes, or until softened. Add the juniper berries and thyme sprigs and return the pork to the pan, with any juices that have collected on the plate. Pour in the cider and stock, season to taste with salt and pepper, then cover and simmer for 30 minutes. Turn the pork over and add the celery. Re-cover the pan and cook for an additional 40 minutes.

Meanwhile, make a beurre manié by mashing the remaining butter with the flour in a small bowl. Transfer the pork and celery to a platter with a slotted spoon and keep warm. Remove and discard the juniper berries and thyme. Whisk the beurre manié, a little at a time, into the simmering cooking liquid. Cook, stirring constantly, for 2 minutes, then stir in the cream and bring to a boil.

Slice the pork and spoon a little of the sauce over it. Garnish with thyme sprigs and serve immediately with the celery, peas, and remaining sauce.

SERVES 4

1 tbsp corn oil

$^1/_4$ cup butter

2 lb 4 oz / 1 kg boned and rolled pork loin

4 shallots, chopped

6 juniper berries

2 fresh thyme sprigs, plus extra to garnish

$^2/_3$ cup hard cider

$^2/_3$ cup chicken stock or water

salt and pepper

8 celery stalks, chopped

2 tbsp all-purpose flour

$^2/_3$ cup heavy cream

freshly cooked peas, to serve

Pork & Vegetable Stew

Trim off any fat or gristle from the pork and cut into thin strips about 2 inches/5 cm long. Mix the flour and spices together. Toss the pork in the spiced flour until well coated and reserve any remaining spiced flour.

Heat the oil in a large, heavy-bottom pan and cook the onion, stirring frequently, for 5 minutes, or until softened. Add the pork and cook over high heat, stirring frequently, for 5 minutes, or until browned on all sides and sealed. Sprinkle in the reserved spiced flour and cook, stirring constantly, for 2 minutes, then remove from the heat.

Gradually add the tomatoes to the pan. Blend the tomato paste with a little of the stock in a pitcher and gradually stir into the pan, then stir in half the remaining stock.

Add the carrots, then return to the heat and bring to a boil, stirring. Reduce the heat, then cover and simmer, stirring occasionally, for 1 1/2 hours. Add the squash and cook for an additional 15 minutes.

Add the leeks and okra, and the remaining stock if you prefer a thinner stew. Simmer for an additional 15 minutes, or until the pork and vegetables are tender. Season to taste with salt and pepper, then garnish with fresh parsley and serve with couscous.

SERVES 4

1 lb/450 g lean boneless pork

1 1/2 tbsp all-purpose flour

1 tsp ground coriander

1 tsp ground cumin

1 1/2 tsp ground cinnamon

1 tbsp olive oil

1 onion, chopped

14 oz/400 g canned chopped tomatoes

2 tbsp tomato paste

1 1/4–scant 2 cups chicken stock

8 oz/225 g carrots, chopped

12 oz/350 g squash, such as kabocha, peeled, seeded, and chopped

8 oz/225 g leeks, sliced, blanched, and drained

4 oz/115 g okra, trimmed and sliced

salt and pepper

sprigs of fresh parsley, to garnish

couscous, to serve

Pork with Red Cabbage

Preheat the oven to 325°F/160°C. Heat the oil in a flameproof casserole. Add the pork and cook over medium heat, turning frequently, for 5–10 minutes, until browned. Transfer to a plate.

Add the chopped onion to the casserole and cook over low heat, stirring occasionally, for 5 minutes, or until softened. Add the cabbage, in batches, and cook, stirring, for 2 minutes. Transfer each batch (mixed with some onion) into a bowl with a slotted spoon.

Add the apple slices, cloves, and sugar to the bowl and mix well, then place about half the mixture in the bottom of the casserole. Top with the pork and add the remaining cabbage mixture. Sprinkle in the lemon juice and add the strip of rind. Cover and cook in the preheated oven for 1 1/2 hours.

Transfer the pork to a plate. Transfer the cabbage mixture to the plate with a slotted spoon and keep warm. Bring the cooking juices to a boil over high heat and reduce slightly. Slice the pork and arrange on warmed serving plates, surrounded with the cabbage mixture. Spoon the cooking juices over the meat and serve with wedges of lemon.

SERVES 4

1 tbsp corn oil

1 lb 10 oz/750 g boned and rolled pork loin

1 onion, finely chopped

1 lb 2 oz/500 g red cabbage, thick stems removed and leaves shredded

2 large cooking apples, peeled, cored, and sliced

3 cloves

1 tsp brown sugar

3 tbsp lemon juice, and a thinly pared strip of lemon rind

lemon wedges, to garnish

Paprika Pork

Cut the pork into 1$\frac{1}{2}$-inch/4-cm cubes. Heat the oil and butter in a large pan. Add the pork and cook over medium heat, stirring, for 5 minutes, or until browned. Transfer to a plate with a slotted spoon.

Add the chopped onion to the pan and cook, stirring occasionally, for 5 minutes, or until softened. Stir in the paprika and flour and cook, stirring constantly, for 2 minutes. Gradually stir in the stock and bring to a boil, stirring constantly.

Return the pork to the pan, add the sherry and sliced mushrooms, and season to taste with salt and pepper. Cover and simmer gently for 20 minutes, or until the pork is tender. Stir in the sour cream and serve.

SERVES 4

1 lb 8 oz/675 g pork tenderloin

2 tbsp corn oil

2 tbsp butter

1 onion, chopped

1 tbsp paprika

2$\frac{1}{2}$ tbsp all-purpose flour

1$\frac{1}{4}$ cups chicken stock

4 tbsp dry sherry

4 oz/115 g button mushrooms, sliced

salt and pepper

$\frac{2}{3}$ cup sour cream

Pork Chops with Bell Peppers & Corn

Heat the oil in a large, flameproof casserole. Add the pork chops in batches and cook over medium heat, turning occasionally, for 5 minutes, or until browned. Transfer the chops to a plate with a slotted spoon.

Add the chopped onion to the casserole and cook, stirring occasionally, for 5 minutes, or until softened. Add the garlic and bell peppers and cook, stirring occasionally, for an additional 5 minutes. Stir in the corn kernels and their juices and the parsley and season to taste.

Return the chops to the casserole, spooning the vegetable mixture over them. Cover and simmer for 30 minutes, or until tender. Serve immediately with mashed potatoes.

SERVES 4

1 tbsp corn oil

4 pork chops, trimmed of visible fat

1 onion, chopped

1 garlic clove, finely chopped

1 green bell pepper, seeded and sliced

1 red bell pepper, seeded and sliced

$11^1/_2$ oz/325 g canned corn kernels

1 tbsp chopped fresh parsley

salt and pepper

mashed potatoes, to serve

Sausage & Bean Casserole

Prick the sausages all over with a fork. Heat 2 tablespoons of the oil in a large, heavy skillet. Add the sausages and cook over low heat, turning frequently, for 10–15 minutes, until evenly browned and cooked through. Remove them from the skillet and keep warm. Drain off the oil and wipe out the skillet with paper towels.

Heat the remaining oil in the skillet. Add the onion, garlic, and bell pepper to the skillet and cook for 5 minutes, stirring occasionally, or until softened.

Add the tomatoes to the skillet and leave the mixture to simmer for about 5 minutes, stirring occasionally, or until slightly reduced and thickened.

Stir the sun-dried tomato paste, cannellini beans, and Italian sausages into the mixture in the skillet. Cook for 4–5 minutes or until the mixture is piping hot. Add 4–5 tablespoons of water, if the mixture becomes too dry during cooking.

Transfer the Italian sausage and bean casserole to serving plates and serve with mashed potatoes or cooked rice.

SERVES 4

8 Italian sausages

3 tbsp olive oil

1 large onion, chopped

2 garlic cloves, chopped

1 green bell pepper, seeded and sliced

8 oz/225 g fresh tomatoes, skinned and chopped or 14 oz/400 g can chopped tomatoes

2 tbsp sun-dried tomato paste

14 oz/400 g can cannellini beans

mashed potatoes or rice, to serve

Asian Pork

Trim off any fat or gristle from the pork and cut into 1-inch/ 2.5-cm chunks. Toss the pork in the flour until well coated and reserve any remaining flour.

Heat the oil in a large, heavy-bottom pan and cook the onion, garlic, and ginger, stirring frequently, for 5 minutes, or until softened. Add the pork and cook over high heat, stirring frequently, for 5 minutes, or until browned on all sides and sealed. Sprinkle in the reserved flour and cook, stirring constantly, for 2 minutes, then remove from the heat.

Blend the tomato paste with the stock in a heatproof pitcher and gradually stir into the pan. Drain the pineapple, reserving both the fruit and juice, and stir the juice into the pan.

Add the soy sauce to the pan, then return to the heat and bring to a boil, stirring. Reduce the heat, then cover and simmer, stirring occasionally, for 1 hour. Add the bell peppers and cook for an additional 15 minutes, or until the pork is tender. Stir in the vinegar and the pineapple and heat through for 5 minutes. Serve sprinkled with the scallions.

SERVES 4

1 lb/450 g lean boneless pork

1$\frac{1}{2}$ tbsp all-purpose flour

1–2 tbsp olive oil

1 onion, cut into small wedges

2–3 garlic cloves, chopped

1-inch/2.5-cm piece fresh gingerroot, peeled and grated

1 tbsp tomato paste

1$\frac{1}{4}$ cups chicken stock

8 oz/225 g canned pineapple chunks in natural juice

1–1$\frac{1}{2}$ tbsp dark soy sauce

1 red bell pepper, seeded and sliced

1 green bell pepper, seeded and sliced

1$\frac{1}{2}$ tbsp balsamic vinegar

4 scallions, diagonally sliced, to garnish

Red Curry Pork with Bell Peppers

Heat the oil in a wok or large skillet and sauté the onion and garlic for 1–2 minutes, until they are softened but not browned.

Add the pork slices and stir-fry for 2–3 minutes until browned all over. Add the bell pepper, mushrooms, and curry paste.

Dissolve the coconut in the stock and add to the wok with the soy sauce. Bring to a boil and let simmer for 4–5 minutes until the liquid has reduced and thickened.

Add the tomatoes and cilantro and cook for 1–2 minutes before serving with noodles or rice.

SERVES 4

2 tbsp vegetable or peanut oil

1 onion, coarsely chopped

2 garlic cloves, chopped

1 lb/450 g pork tenderloin, sliced thickly

1 red bell pepper, seeded and cut into squares

6 oz/175 g button mushrooms, quartered

2 tbsp Thai red curry paste

4 oz/115 g block creamed coconut, chopped

1$\frac{1}{4}$ cups pork or vegetable stock

2 tbsp Thai soy sauce

4 tomatoes, peeled, seeded, and chopped

handful of fresh cilantro, chopped

boiled noodles or rice, to serve

Venison Casserole

Preheat the oven to 350°F/180°C. Heat the oil in a large, flameproof casserole and cook the venison over high heat, stirring frequently, for 5 minutes, or until browned on all sides and sealed. Transfer to a large plate using a slotted spoon.

Add the onion and garlic to the casserole and cook over medium heat, stirring frequently, for 5 minutes, or until softened. Transfer to the plate with the meat.

Gradually stir in the stock and scrape any sediment from the bottom of the casserole, then bring to a boil, stirring.

Sprinkle the flour over the meat, onions, and garlic on the plate, and toss well to coat evenly. Return to the casserole and stir well, ensuring that the meat is just covered with the stock. Stir in the wine, redcurrant jelly, and spices.

Season well with salt and pepper, then cover and cook in the center of the preheated oven for 2–2½ hours.

Check and adjust the seasoning if necessary, then serve piping hot with baked or mashed potatoes.

SERVES 6

3 tbsp olive oil

2 lb 4 oz/1 kg casserole venison, cut into 1¼-inch/3-cm cubes

2 onions, finely sliced

2 garlic cloves, chopped

1½ cups beef stock or vegetable stock

2 tbsp all-purpose flour

½ cup port or red wine

2 tbsp redcurrant jelly

6 juniper berries, crushed

4 cloves, crushed

pinch of cinnamon

small grating of nutmeg

salt and pepper

baked or mashed potatoes, to serve

Poultry Pot Wonders

One-pot cooking is the perfect technique for poultry, especially chicken, which can sometimes be disappointingly bland and dry when cooked in other ways. Fabulous stews and aromatic curries burst with flavor and there's even a recipe for an all-in-one classic roast chicken with none of the classic hassle. Discover the versatility of poultry and explore the ease of one-pot cooking with these inspiring international recipes for chicken, turkey, and duck.

Chicken & Barley Stew

Heat the oil in a large pot over medium heat. Add the chicken and cook for 3 minutes, then turn over and cook on the other side for another 2 minutes. Add the stock, barley, potatoes, carrots, leek, shallots, tomato paste, and bay leaf. Bring to a boil, lower the heat, and simmer for 30 minutes.

Add the zucchini and chopped parsley, cover the pan, and cook for another 20 minutes, or until the chicken is cooked through. Remove the bay leaf and discard.

In a separate bowl, mix the flour with 4 tablespoons of water and stir into a smooth paste. Add it to the stew and cook, stirring, over low heat for another 5 minutes. Season to taste with salt and pepper.

Remove from the heat, ladle into individual serving bowls, and garnish with sprigs of fresh parsley. Serve with fresh crusty bread.

SERVES 4

2 tbsp vegetable oil

8 small, skinless chicken thighs

generous 2 cups chicken stock

scant $^1/_2$ cup pearl barley, rinsed and drained

7 oz/200 g small new potatoes, scrubbed and cut in half lengthwise

2 large carrots, peeled and sliced

1 leek, trimmed and sliced

2 shallots, sliced

1 tbsp tomato paste

1 bay leaf

1 zucchini, trimmed and sliced

2 tbsp chopped fresh flat-leaf parsley, plus extra sprigs to garnish

2 tbsp all-purpose flour

salt and pepper

fresh crusty bread, to serve

Coq au Vin

Melt half the butter with the olive oil in a large, flameproof casserole. Add the chicken and cook over medium heat, stirring, for 8–10 minutes, or until golden brown. Add the bacon, onions, mushrooms, and garlic.

Pour in the brandy and set it alight with a match or taper. When the flames have died down, add the wine, stock, and bouquet garni and season to taste with salt and pepper. Bring to a boil, reduce the heat, and simmer gently for 1 hour, or until the chicken pieces are cooked through and tender. Meanwhile, make a beurre manié by mashing the remaining butter with the flour in a small bowl.

Remove and discard the bouquet garni. Transfer the chicken to a large plate and keep warm. Stir the beurre manié into the casserole, a little at a time. Bring to a boil, return the chicken to the casserole, and serve immediately, garnished with bay leaves.

SERVES 4

$^1/_4$ cup butter

2 tbsp olive oil

4 lb/1.8 kg chicken pieces

4 oz/115 g rindless smoked bacon, cut into strips

4 oz/115 g pearl onions, peeled

4 oz/115 g cremini mushrooms, halved

2 garlic cloves, finely chopped

2 tbsp brandy

scant 1 cup red wine

$1^1/_4$ cups chicken stock

1 bouquet garni

salt and pepper

2 tbsp all-purpose flour

bay leaves, to garnish

Classic Roast Chicken

Rinse the chicken inside and out with cold water and drain well. Carefully cut between the skin and the top of the breast meat using a small pointed knife. Slide a finger into the slit and carefully enlarge it to form a pocket. Continue until the skin is completely lifted away from both breasts and the top of the legs.

Chop the leaves from 3 rosemary stems. Mix with the feta cheese, sun-dried tomato paste, butter, and pepper to taste, then spoon under the skin. Put the chicken in a large roasting pan, cover with foil and cook in a preheated oven, 375°F/190°C, for 20 minutes per 1 lb 2 oz/500 g, plus 20 minutes.

Break the garlic bulb into cloves but do not peel. Add the vegetables and garlic to the chicken after 40 minutes.

Drizzle with oil, tuck in a few stems of rosemary, and season with salt and pepper. Cook for the remaining calculated time, removing the foil for the last 40 minutes to brown the chicken.

Transfer the chicken to a serving platter. Place some of the vegetables around the chicken and transfer the remainder to a warmed serving dish. Spoon the fat (it will be floating on top) out of the roasting pan and stir the flour into the remaining cooking juices. Place the roasting pan on top of the stove and cook over medium heat for 2 minutes, then gradually stir in the stock. Bring to a boil, stirring until thickened. Strain into a sauce boat and serve with the chicken.

SERVES 6

5 lb 8 oz/2.5 kg chicken

sprigs of fresh rosemary

$^3/_4$ cup feta cheese, coarsely grated

2 tbsp sun-dried tomato paste

4 tbsp butter, softened

salt and pepper

1 bulb garlic

2 lb 4 oz/1 kg new potatoes, halved if large

1 each red, green, and yellow bell pepper, seeded and cut into chunks

3 zucchini, thinly sliced

2 tbsp olive oil

2 tbsp all-purpose flour

2$^1/_2$ cups chicken stock

Spicy Aromatic Chicken

Rub the chicken pieces with the lemon. Heat the oil in a large flameproof casserole or lidded skillet. Add the onion and garlic and cook for 5 minutes, until softened. Add the chicken pieces and cook for 5–10 minutes, until browned on all sides.

Pour in the wine and add the tomatoes with their juice, the sugar, cinnamon, cloves, allspice, salt, and pepper and bring to a boil. Cover the casserole and simmer for 45 minutes to 1 hour, until the chicken is tender.

Meanwhile, if using artichoke hearts, cut them in half. Add the artichokes or okra and the olives to the casserole 10 minutes before the end of cooking, and continue to simmer until heated through. Serve hot.

SERVES 4

4–8 chicken pieces, skinned

$1/2$ lemon, cut into wedges

4 tbsp olive oil

1 onion, coarsely chopped

2 large garlic cloves, finely chopped

$1/2$ cup dry white wine

14 oz/400 g canned chopped
   tomatoes in juice

pinch of sugar

$1/2$ tsp ground cinnamon

$1/2$ tsp ground cloves

$1/2$ tsp ground allspice

salt and pepper

14 oz/400 g canned artichoke
   hearts or okra, drained

8 black olives, pitted

Brunswick Stew

Season the chicken pieces with salt and dust with paprika.

Heat the oil and butter in a flameproof casserole or large pan. Add the chicken pieces and cook over medium heat, turning, for 10–15 minutes, or until golden. Transfer to a plate with a slotted spoon.

Add the onions and bell peppers to the casserole. Cook over low heat, stirring occasionally, for 5 minutes, or until softened. Add the tomatoes, wine, stock, Worcestershire sauce, Tabasco sauce, and parsley and bring to a boil, stirring. Return the chicken to the casserole, cover, and simmer, stirring occasionally, for 30 minutes.

Add the corn and beans to the casserole, partially re-cover, and simmer for an additional 30 minutes. Place the flour and water in a small bowl and mix to make a paste. Stir a ladleful of the cooking liquid into the paste, then stir it into the stew. Cook, stirring frequently, for 5 minutes. Serve, garnished with parsley.

SERVES 6

4 lb / 1.8 kg chicken pieces

salt

2 tbsp paprika

2 tbsp olive oil

2 tbsp butter

1 lb / 450 g onions, chopped

2 yellow bell peppers, seeded and chopped

14 oz / 400 g canned chopped tomatoes

scant 1 cup dry white wine

generous $1^3/_4$ cups chicken stock

1 tbsp Worcestershire sauce

$^1/_2$ tsp Tabasco sauce

1 tbsp finely chopped fresh parsley

$11^1/_2$ oz / 325 g canned corn kernels, drained

15 oz / 425 g canned lima beans, drained and rinsed

2 tbsp all-purpose flour

4 tbsp water

fresh parsley sprigs, to garnish

Chicken in White Wine

Preheat the oven to 325°F/160°C. Melt half the butter with the oil in a flameproof casserole. Add the bacon and cook over medium heat, stirring, for 5–10 minutes, or until golden brown. Transfer the bacon to a large plate. Add the onions and garlic to the casserole and cook over low heat, stirring occasionally, for 10 minutes, or until golden. Transfer to the plate. Add the chicken and cook over medium heat, stirring constantly, for 8–10 minutes, or until golden. Transfer to the plate.

Drain off any excess fat from the casserole. Stir in the wine and stock and bring to a boil, scraping any sediment off the bottom. Add the bouquet garni and season to taste. Return the bacon, onions, and chicken to the casserole. Cover and cook in the preheated oven for 1 hour. Add the mushrooms, re-cover, and cook for 15 minutes. Meanwhile, make a beurre manié by mashing the remaining butter with the flour in a small bowl.

Remove the casserole from the oven and set over medium heat. Remove and discard the bouquet garni. Whisk in the beurre manié, a little at a time. Bring to a boil, stirring constantly, then serve, garnished with fresh herb sprigs.

SERVES 4

$1/4$ cup butter

2 tbsp olive oil

2 thick, rindless, lean bacon strips, chopped

4 oz/115 g pearl onions, peeled

1 garlic clove, finely chopped

4 lb/1.8 kg chicken pieces

$1^3/4$ cups dry white wine

$1^1/4$ cups chicken stock

1 bouquet garni

salt and pepper

4 oz/115 g button mushrooms

$2^1/2$ tbsp all-purpose flour

fresh herb sprigs, to garnish

Hunter's Chicken

Preheat the oven to 325°F/160°C. Heat the butter and oil in a flameproof casserole and cook the chicken over medium-high heat, turning frequently, for 10 minutes, or until golden all over and sealed. Using a slotted spoon, transfer to a plate.

Add the onions and garlic to the casserole and cook over low heat, stirring occasionally, for 10 minutes, or until softened and golden. Add the tomatoes with their juice, the herbs, sun-dried tomato paste, and wine, and season to taste with salt and pepper. Bring to a boil, then return the chicken portions to the casserole, pushing them down into the sauce.

Cover and cook in the preheated oven for 50 minutes. Add the mushrooms and cook for an additional 10 minutes, or until the chicken is tender and the juices run clear when a skewer is inserted into the thickest part of the meat. Serve immediately.

SERVES 4

1 tbsp unsalted butter

2 tbsp olive oil

4 lb/1.8 kg skinned, unboned chicken portions

2 red onions, sliced

2 garlic cloves, finely chopped

14 oz/400 g canned chopped tomatoes

2 tbsp chopped fresh flat-leaf parsley

6 fresh basil leaves, torn

1 tbsp sun-dried tomato paste

$^2/_3$ cup red wine

salt and pepper

8 oz/225 g button mushrooms, sliced

Florida Chicken

Lightly rinse the chicken and pat dry with paper towels. Cut into bite-size pieces. Season the flour well with salt and pepper. Toss the chicken in the seasoned flour until well coated and reserve any remaining seasoned flour.

Heat the oil in a large, heavy-bottom skillet and cook the chicken over high heat, stirring frequently, for 5 minutes, or until golden on all sides and sealed. Using a slotted spoon, transfer to a plate.

Add the onion and celery to the skillet and cook over medium heat, stirring frequently, for 5 minutes, or until softened. Sprinkle in the reserved seasoned flour and cook, stirring constantly, for 2 minutes, then remove from the heat. Gradually stir in the orange juice, stock, soy sauce, and honey followed by the orange rind, then return to the heat and bring to a boil, stirring.

Return the chicken to the skillet. Reduce the heat, then cover and simmer, stirring occasionally, for 15 minutes. Add the orange bell pepper, zucchini, and corn cobs and simmer for an additional 10 minutes, or until the chicken and vegetables are tender. Add the orange segments, then stir well and heat through for 1 minute. Serve garnished with the parsley.

SERVES 4

1 lb/450 g skinless, boneless chicken

$1^1/_2$ tbsp all-purpose flour

salt and pepper

1 tbsp olive oil

1 onion, cut into wedges

2 celery stalks, sliced

$^2/_3$ cup orange juice

$1^1/_4$ cups chicken stock

1 tbsp light soy sauce

1–2 tsp clear honey

1 tbsp grated orange rind

1 orange bell pepper, seeded and chopped

8 oz/225 g zucchini, sliced into half moons

2 small corn cobs, halved, or $3^1/_2$ oz/100 g baby corn

1 orange, peeled and segmented

1 tbsp chopped fresh parsley, to garnish

Thai Green Chicken Curry

First make the curry paste. Seed the chiles if you like and coarsely chop. Place all the paste ingredients, except the oil, in a mortar and pound with a pestle. Alternatively, process in a food processor. Gradually blend in the oil.

Heat the remaining 2 tablespoons of oil in a preheated wok or large, heavy-bottom skillet. Add 2 tablespoons of the curry paste and stir-fry briefly until all the aromas are released.

Add the chicken, lime leaves, and lemongrass and stir-fry for 3–4 minutes, until the meat is starting to color. Add the coconut milk and eggplants and let simmer gently for 8–10 minutes, or until tender.

Stir in the fish sauce and serve at once, garnished with Thai basil sprigs and lime leaves.

SERVES 4

2 tbsp peanut or corn oil

1 lb 2 oz/500 g skinless boneless chicken breasts, cut into cubes

2 kaffir lime leaves, coarsely torn

1 lemongrass stalk, finely chopped

1 cup canned coconut milk

16 baby eggplants, halved

2 tbsp Thai fish sauce

fresh Thai basil sprigs and thinly sliced kaffir lime leaves, to garnish

for the green curry paste

16 fresh green chiles

2 shallots, sliced

4 kaffir lime leaves

1 lemongrass stalk, chopped

2 garlic cloves, chopped

1 tsp cumin seeds

1 tsp coriander seeds

1 tbsp grated fresh gingerroot or galangal

1 tsp grated lime rind

5 black peppercorns

1 tbsp sugar

salt

2 tbsp peanut or corn oil

Chicken Tagine

Heat the oil in a large pan over medium heat, add the onion and garlic and cook for 3 minutes, stirring frequently. Add the chicken and cook, stirring constantly, for an additional 5 minutes, or until sealed on all sides. Add the cumin and cinnamon sticks to the pan halfway through sealing the chicken.

Sprinkle in the flour and cook, stirring constantly, for 2 minutes.

Add the eggplant, red bell pepper, and mushrooms and cook for an additional 2 minutes, stirring constantly.

Blend the tomato paste with the stock, stir into the pan, and bring to a boil. Reduce the heat and add the chickpeas and apricots. Cover and let simmer for 15–20 minutes, or until the chicken is tender.

Season with salt and pepper to taste and serve at once, sprinkled with cilantro.

SERVES 4

1 tbsp olive oil

1 onion, cut into small wedges

2–4 garlic cloves, sliced

1 lb/450 g skinless, boneless chicken breast, diced

1 tsp ground cumin

2 cinnamon sticks, lightly bruised

1 tbsp whole wheat flour

8 oz/225 g eggplant, diced

1 red bell pepper, seeded and chopped

3 oz/85 g button mushrooms, sliced

1 tbsp tomato paste

$2^1/2$ cups chicken stock

10 oz/280 g canned chickpeas, drained and rinsed

$^1/_3$ cup chopped no-soak apricots

salt and pepper

1 tbsp chopped fresh cilantro

Chicken Jalfrezi

Grind the cumin and coriander seeds in a mortar with a pestle, then reserve. Heat the mustard oil in a large, heavy-bottom pan over high heat for 1 minute, or until it begins to smoke. Add the vegetable oil, reduce the heat, and add the onion and garlic. Cook for 10 minutes, or until golden.

Add the tomato paste, chopped tomatoes, turmeric, ground cumin and coriander seeds, chili powder, garam masala, and vinegar to the skillet. Stir the mixture until fragrant.

Add the red bell pepper and fava beans and stir for an additional 2 minutes, or until the bell pepper is softened. Stir in the chicken, and season to taste with salt, then simmer gently for 6–8 minutes, until the chicken is heated through and the beans are tender. Transfer to warmed serving bowls, garnish with cilantro sprigs, and serve with freshly cooked rice.

SERVES 4

$^1/_2$ tsp cumin seeds

$^1/_2$ tsp coriander seeds

1 tsp mustard oil

3 tbsp vegetable oil

1 large onion, finely chopped

3 garlic cloves, crushed

1 tbsp tomato paste

2 tomatoes, peeled and chopped

1 tsp ground turmeric

$^1/_2$ tsp chili powder

$^1/_2$ tsp garam masala

1 tsp red wine vinegar

1 small red bell pepper, seeded
  and chopped

$4^1/_2$ oz/125 g frozen fava beans

1 lb 2 oz/500 g cooked chicken,
  chopped

salt

fresh cilantro sprigs, to garnish

freshly cooked rice, to serve

Balti Chicken

Heat the ghee in a large, heavy-bottom skillet. Add the onions and cook over low heat, stirring occasionally, for 10 minutes, or until golden. Add the sliced tomatoes, nigella seeds, peppercorns, cardamom, cinnamon stick, chili powder, garam masala, garlic paste, and ginger paste and season with salt to taste. Cook, stirring constantly, for 5 minutes.

Add the chicken and cook, stirring constantly, for 5 minutes, or until well coated in the spice paste. Stir in the yogurt. Cover and let simmer, stirring occasionally, for 10 minutes.

Stir in the chopped cilantro, chiles, and lime juice. Transfer to a warmed serving dish, sprinkle with more chopped cilantro, and serve immediately.

SERVES 6

3 tbsp ghee or vegetable oil

2 large onions, sliced

3 tomatoes, sliced

$^1/_2$ tsp nigella seeds

4 black peppercorns

2 cardamom pods

1 cinnamon stick

1 tsp chili powder

1 tsp garam masala

1 tsp garlic paste

1 tsp ginger paste

salt

1 lb 9 oz/700 g skinless, boneless chicken breasts or thighs, diced

2 tbsp plain yogurt

2 tbsp chopped fresh cilantro, plus extra to garnish

2 fresh green chiles, seeded and finely chopped

2 tbsp lime juice

Chicken with Garlic

Sift the flour onto a large plate and season with paprika and salt and pepper to taste. Dredge the chicken pieces with the flour on both sides, shaking off the excess.

Heat 4 tablespoons of the oil in a large, deep skillet or flameproof casserole over medium heat. Add the garlic and cook, stirring frequently, for about 2 minutes to flavor the oil. Remove with a slotted spoon and set aside to drain on paper towels.

Add as many chicken pieces, skin-side down, as will fit in a single layer. (Work in batches to avoid overcrowding the skillet, adding a little extra oil if necessary.) Cook for 5 minutes until the skin is golden brown. Turn over and cook for 5 minutes longer.

Pour off any excess oil. Return the garlic and chicken pieces to the skillet and add the chicken stock, wine, and herbs. Bring to a boil, then reduce the heat, cover, and let simmer for 20–25 minutes until the chicken is cooked through and tender and the garlic is very soft.

Transfer the chicken pieces to a serving platter and keep warm. Bring the cooking liquid to a boil, with the garlic and herbs, and boil until reduced to about 1½ cups. Remove and discard the herbs. Taste and adjust the seasoning, if necessary.

Spoon the sauce and the garlic cloves over the chicken pieces. Garnish with the parsley and thyme, and serve.

SERVES 4

4 tbsp all-purpose flour

Spanish paprika, either hot or
  smoked sweet, to taste

salt and pepper

1 large chicken, about 3 lb 12 oz/
  1.75 kg, cut into 8 pieces, rinsed,
  and patted dry

4–6 tbsp olive oil

24 large garlic cloves, peeled and
  halved

scant 2 cups chicken stock,
  preferably homemade

4 tbsp dry white wine, such as
  white Rioja

2 sprigs of fresh parsley, 1 bay leaf,
  and 1 sprig of fresh thyme, tied
  together

fresh parsley and thyme leaves,
  to garnish

Louisiana Chicken

Heat the oil in a large, heavy-bottom pan or flameproof casserole. Add the chicken and cook over medium heat, stirring, for 5–10 minutes, or until golden. Transfer the chicken to a plate with a slotted spoon.

Stir the flour into the oil and cook over very low heat, stirring constantly, for 15 minutes, or until light golden. Do not let it burn. Immediately, add the onion, celery, and green bell pepper and cook, stirring constantly, for 2 minutes. Add the garlic, thyme, and chiles and cook, stirring, for 1 minute.

Stir in the tomatoes and their juices, then gradually stir in the stock. Return the chicken pieces to the pan, cover, and simmer for 45 minutes, or until the chicken is cooked through and tender. Season to taste with salt and pepper, transfer to warmed serving plates and serve immediately, garnished with some corn salad and a sprinkling of chopped thyme.

SERVES 4

5 tbsp corn oil

4 chicken portions

6 tbsp all-purpose flour

1 onion, chopped

2 celery stalks, sliced

1 green bell pepper, seeded
and chopped

2 garlic cloves, finely chopped

2 tsp chopped fresh thyme

2 fresh red chiles, seeded
and finely chopped

14 oz/400 g canned chopped
tomatoes

1¼ cups chicken stock

salt and pepper

to garnish

corn salad

chopped fresh thyme

Chicken Pepperonata

Toss the chicken thighs in the flour, shaking off the excess.

Heat the oil in a wide skillet and cook the chicken quickly until sealed and lightly browned, then remove from the pan.

Add the onion to the pan and gently cook until soft. Add the garlic, bell peppers, tomatoes, and oregano, then bring to a boil, stirring.

Arrange the chicken over the vegetables, season well with salt and pepper, then cover the pan tightly and simmer for 20–25 minutes or until the chicken is completely cooked and tender.

Taste and adjust the seasoning if necessary, garnish with oregano, and serve with crusty whole wheat bread.

SERVES 4

8 skinless chicken thighs

2 tbsp whole wheat flour

2 tbsp olive oil

1 small onion, thinly sliced

1 garlic clove, crushed

1 each large red, yellow, and
   green bell peppers, seeded and
   thinly sliced

14 oz/400 g can chopped tomatoes

1 tbsp chopped fresh oregano,
   plus extra to garnish

salt and pepper

crusty whole wheat bread, to serve

Mexican Chicken, Chile & Potato Pot

Heat the oil in a large, heavy pan over medium-high heat. Cook the chicken until lightly browned.

Reduce the heat to medium. Add the onion, bell pepper, potato, and sweet potato. Cover and cook for 5 minutes, stirring occasionally, until the vegetables begin to soften.

Add the garlic and chiles. Cook for 1 minute. Stir in the tomatoes, oregano, salt, pepper, and 2 tablespoons of the cilantro. Cook for 1 minute.

Pour in the stock. Bring to a boil, then cover, and simmer over medium-low heat for 15–20 minutes, or until the chicken is cooked through and the vegetables are tender. Sprinkle with the remaining cilantro just before serving.

SERVES 4

2 tbsp vegetable oil

1 lb/450 g boneless, skinless chicken breasts, cubed

1 onion, finely chopped

1 green bell pepper, seeded and finely chopped

1 potato, diced

1 sweet potato, diced

2 garlic cloves, very finely chopped

1–2 green chiles, seeded and very finely chopped

7 oz/200 g canned chopped tomatoes

½ tsp dried oregano

½ tsp salt

¼ tsp pepper

4 tbsp chopped fresh cilantro

2 cups chicken stock

Chicken Basquaise

Pat the chicken pieces dry with paper towels. Put the flour in a plastic bag, season with salt and pepper, and add the chicken pieces. Seal the bag and shake to coat the chicken.

Heat 2 tablespoons of the oil in a large flameproof casserole over medium-high heat. Add the chicken and cook, turning frequently, for about 15 minutes until well browned all over. Transfer to a plate.

Heat the remaining oil in the casserole and add the onion and bell peppers. Reduce the heat to medium and stir-fry until beginning to color and soften. Add the garlic, chorizo, and tomato paste and cook, stirring constantly, for about 3 minutes. Add the rice and cook, stirring to coat, for about 2 minutes until the rice is translucent.

Add the stock, chile flakes, and thyme, season to taste with salt and pepper, and stir well. Bring to a boil. Return the chicken to the casserole, pressing it gently into the rice. Cover and cook over very low heat for about 45 minutes until the chicken is cooked through and the rice is tender.

Gently stir the prosciutto, black olives, and half the parsley into the rice mixture. Re-cover and heat through for an additional 5 minutes. Sprinkle with the remaining parsley and serve immediately.

SERVES 4–5

1 chicken, weighing 3 lb/1.35 kg, cut into 8 pieces

2 tbsp all-purpose flour

salt and pepper

3 tbsp olive oil

1 Bermuda onion, thickly sliced

2 red or yellow bell peppers, seeded and cut lengthwise into thick strips

2 garlic cloves

5$\frac{1}{2}$ oz/150 g spicy chorizo sausage, peeled and cut into $\frac{1}{2}$-inch/1-cm pieces

1 tbsp tomato paste

1 cup long-grain white rice

2 cups chicken stock

1 tsp chile flakes

$\frac{1}{2}$ tsp dried thyme

$\frac{3}{4}$ cup diced prosciutto

12 dry-cured black olives

2 tbsp chopped fresh flat-leaf parsley

Chicken with Rice, Mushrooms & Tomatoes

Heat the oil in a large, heavy skillet over medium-high heat. Cook the chicken until lightly browned, stirring frequently.

Reduce the heat to medium. Add the onion and mushrooms. Cook for 5 minutes, or until soft. Stir in the garlic and 2 tablespoons of the parsley. Cook for 1 minute. Add the rice and cook for 5 minutes, stirring constantly. Add the tomatoes. Season with salt and pepper. Cook for another minute.

Stir in the hot stock. Bring to a boil, then cover tightly, and simmer over low heat for 20–25 minutes, or until the rice is tender.

Remove from the heat and let the dish stand, covered, for 10 minutes before serving. Sprinkle with the remaining parsley to garnish and serve.

SERVES 4

2 tbsp olive oil

1 lb 7 oz/650 g boneless, skinless chicken breasts, cubed

1 onion, finely chopped

1 cup finely sliced button mushrooms

2 garlic cloves, very finely chopped

4 tbsp chopped fresh flat-leaf parsley

1¾ cups long-grain rice

14 oz/400 g canned chopped tomatoes

salt and pepper

2 cups chicken stock

Chicken Risotto with Saffron

Melt 2 oz/55 g of the butter in a deep pan, add the chicken and onion and cook, stirring frequently, for 8 minutes, or until golden brown.

Add the rice and mix to coat in the butter. Cook, stirring constantly for 2–3 minutes, or until the grains are translucent. Add the wine and cook, stirring constantly, for 1 minute until reduced.

Mix the saffron with 4 tablespoons of the hot stock. Add the liquid to the rice and cook, stirring constantly, until it is absorbed.

Gradually add the remaining hot stock, a ladleful at a time. Stir constantly and add more liquid as the rice absorbs each addition. Cook for 20 minutes, or until all the liquid is absorbed and the rice is creamy. Season to taste.

Remove the risotto from the heat and add the remaining butter. Mix well, then stir in the Parmesan until it melts. Spoon the risotto onto warmed plates and serve at once.

SERVES 4

$4^{1}/_{2}$ oz/125 g butter

2 lb/900 g skinless, boneless chicken breasts, thinly sliced

1 large onion, chopped

1 lb 2 oz/500 g risotto rice

$^{2}/_{3}$ cup white wine

1 tsp crumbled saffron threads

generous $5^{1}/_{2}$ cups boiling chicken stock

salt and pepper

$^{1}/_{2}$ cup freshly grated Parmesan cheese

Mexican Turkey

Preheat the oven to 325°F/160°C. Spread the flour on a plate and season with salt and pepper. Coat the turkey fillets in the seasoned flour, shaking off any excess.

Heat the oil in a flameproof casserole. Add the turkey fillets and cook over medium heat, turning occasionally, for 5–10 minutes, or until golden. Transfer to a plate with a slotted spoon.

Add the onion and bell pepper to the casserole. Cook over low heat, stirring occasionally, for 5 minutes, or until softened. Sprinkle in any remaining seasoned flour and cook, stirring constantly, for 1 minute. Gradually stir in the stock, then add the raisins, chopped tomatoes, chili powder, cinnamon, cumin, and chocolate. Season to taste with salt and pepper. Bring to a boil, stirring constantly.

Return the turkey to the casserole, cover, and cook in the preheated oven for 50 minutes. Serve immediately, garnished with sprigs of cilantro.

SERVES 4

6 tbsp all-purpose flour

salt and pepper

4 turkey breast fillets

3 tbsp corn oil

1 onion, thinly sliced

1 red bell pepper, seeded and sliced

$1^{1}/_{4}$ cups chicken stock

2 tbsp raisins

4 tomatoes, peeled, seeded,
   and chopped

1 tsp chili powder

$^{1}/_{2}$ tsp ground cinnamon

pinch of ground cumin

1 oz/25 g semisweet chocolate,
   finely chopped or grated

sprigs of fresh cilantro, to garnish

Italian Turkey Steaks

Heat the oil in a flameproof casserole or heavy-bottom skillet. Add the turkey scallops and cook over medium heat for 5–10 minutes, turning occasionally, until golden. Transfer to a plate.

Seed and slice the red bell peppers. Slice the onion, add to the skillet with the bell peppers, and cook over low heat, stirring occasionally, for 5 minutes, or until softened. Add the garlic and cook for an additional 2 minutes. Return the turkey to the skillet and add the strained tomatoes, wine, and marjoram. Season to taste. Bring to a boil, then reduce the heat, cover, and simmer, stirring occasionally, for 25–30 minutes, or until the turkey is cooked through and tender.

Stir in the cannellini beans. Simmer for an additional 5 minutes. Sprinkle the breadcrumbs over the top and place under a preheated medium-hot broiler for 2–3 minutes, or until golden. Serve, garnished with basil.

SERVES 4

1 tbsp olive oil

4 turkey scallops or steaks

2 red bell peppers

1 red onion

2 garlic cloves, finely chopped

$1^{1}/_{4}$ cups strained tomatoes

$^{2}/_{3}$ cup medium white wine

1 tbsp chopped fresh marjoram

salt and pepper

14 oz/400 g canned cannellini beans, drained and rinsed

3 tbsp fresh white breadcrumbs

fresh basil sprigs, to garnish

Duck Legs with Olives

Put the duck legs in the bottom of a flameproof casserole or a large, heavy-bottom skillet with a tight-fitting lid. Add the tomatoes, garlic, onion, carrot, celery, thyme, and olives, and stir together. Season with salt and pepper to taste.

Turn the heat to high and cook, uncovered, until the ingredients start to bubble. Reduce the heat to low, cover tightly, and let simmer for 1¼–1½ hours until the duck is very tender. Check occasionally and add a little water if the mixture appears to be drying out.

When the duck is tender, transfer it to a serving platter, cover, and keep hot in a preheated warm oven. Leave the casserole uncovered, increase the heat to medium, and cook, stirring, for about 10 minutes until the mixture forms a sauce. Stir in the orange rind, then taste and adjust the seasoning if necessary.

Mash the tender garlic cloves with a fork and spread over the duck legs. Spoon the sauce over the top. Serve at once.

SERVES 4

4 duck legs, all visible fat trimmed off

1 lb 12 oz/800 g canned tomatoes, chopped

8 garlic cloves, peeled, but left whole

1 large onion, chopped

1 carrot, finely chopped

1 celery stalk, finely chopped

3 sprigs fresh thyme

generous ½ cup Spanish green olives in brine, stuffed with pimientos, garlic, or almonds, drained and rinsed

salt and pepper

1 tsp finely grated orange rind

Duck Jambalaya-style Stew

Remove and discard the skin and any fat from the duck breasts. Cut the flesh into bite-size pieces.

Heat the oil in a large deep skillet and cook the duck, ham, and chorizo over high heat, stirring frequently, for 5 minutes, or until browned on all sides and sealed. Using a slotted spoon, remove from the skillet and set aside.

Add the onion, garlic, celery, and chiles to the skillet and cook over medium heat, stirring frequently, for 5 minutes, or until softened. Add the green bell pepper, then stir in the stock, oregano, tomatoes, and hot pepper sauce.

Bring to a boil, then reduce the heat and return the duck, ham, and chorizo to the skillet. Cover and simmer, stirring occasionally, for 20 minutes, or until the duck and ham are tender.

Serve immediately, garnished with parsley and accompanied by salad greens and rice.

SERVES 4

4 duck breasts, about $5^{1}/_{2}$ oz/ 150 g each

2 tbsp olive oil

8 oz/225 g piece ham, cut into small chunks

8 oz/225 g chorizo, outer casing removed

1 onion, chopped

3 garlic cloves, chopped

3 celery stalks, chopped

1–2 fresh red chiles, seeded and chopped

1 green bell pepper, seeded and chopped

$2^{1}/_{2}$ cups chicken stock

1 tbsp chopped fresh oregano

14 oz/400 g canned chopped tomatoes

1–2 tsp hot pepper sauce, or to taste

chopped fresh parsley, to garnish

to serve

salad greens

freshly cooked long-grain rice

Braised Asian Duck

Combine 1 tablespoon of the soy sauce, the five-spice powder, pepper, and salt and rub over the duck pieces. Heat 2½ tablespoons of the vegetable oil in a flameproof casserole, add the duck pieces, and cook over a medium heat, stirring, until browned. Transfer to a plate with a slotted spoon.

Drain the fat from the casserole and wipe out with paper towels. Heat the sesame oil and remaining vegetable oil. Add the ginger and garlic. Cook for a few seconds. Add the white scallions. Cook for a few seconds.

Return the duck to the pan. Add the rice wine, oyster sauce, star anise, peppercorns, and remaining soy sauce. Pour in just enough stock to cover. Bring to a boil, cover, and simmer gently for 1½ hours, adding more water if necessary.

Drain the mushrooms and squeeze dry. Slice the caps and add to the duck with the water chestnuts. Simmer for 20 minutes more.

Mix the cornstarch with 2 tablespoons of the cooking liquid to a smooth paste. Add to the remaining liquid, stirring until thickened. Garnish with the green scallion shreds to serve.

SERVES 4

3 tbsp soy sauce

¼ tsp Chinese five-spice powder

¼ tsp pepper

pinch of salt

4 duck legs or breasts, cut into pieces

3 tbsp vegetable oil

1 tsp dark sesame oil

1 tsp finely chopped fresh gingerroot

1 large garlic clove, finely chopped

4 scallions, white part thickly sliced, green part shredded

2 tbsp rice wine or dry sherry

1 tbsp oyster sauce

3 whole star anise

2 tsp black peppercorns

2–2½ cups chicken stock or water

6 dried shiitake mushrooms, soaked in warm water for 20 minutes

8 oz/225 g canned water chestnuts, drained and rinsed

2 tbsp cornstarch

4

Fish & Seafood Suppers

From fiery fish curries to rich Mediterranean seafood stews and from mussels to swordfish, these recipes prove once and for all that cooking—and eating—fish is not a chore but a pleasure. Even fussy children will be intrigued to open up tasty little fish packages baked in the oven. Classic fish and seafood dishes are the perfect choice for easy and impressive entertaining, while roasted fish will prove to be a revelation even to confirmed meat-eaters.

Spanish Fish Stew

Put the saffron threads in a heatproof pitcher with the water and let stand for at least 10 minutes to infuse.

Heat the oil in a large, heavy-bottom flameproof casserole over medium-high heat. Reduce the heat to low and cook the onion, stirring occasionally, for 10 minutes, or until golden but not browned. Stir in the garlic, thyme, bay leaves, and red bell peppers and cook, stirring frequently, for 5 minutes, or until the bell peppers are softened and the onions have softened further. Add the tomatoes and paprika and simmer, stirring frequently, for an additional 5 minutes.

Stir in the stock, the saffron and its soaking liquid, and the almonds and bring to a boil, stirring. Reduce the heat and simmer for 5–10 minutes, or until the sauce reduces and thickens. Season to taste with salt and pepper.

Meanwhile, clean the mussels and clams by scrubbing or scraping the shells and pulling out any beards that are attached to the mussels. Discard any with broken shells or any that refuse to close when tapped.

Gently stir the hake into the stew so that it doesn't break up, then add the shrimp, mussels, and clams. Reduce the heat to very low, then cover and simmer for 5 minutes, or until the hake is opaque, the mussels and clams have opened, and the shrimp have turned pink. Discard any mussels or clams that remain closed. Serve immediately with plenty of thick crusty bread for soaking up the juices.

SERVES 4–6

large pinch of saffron threads

4 tbsp almost boiling water

6 tbsp olive oil

1 large onion, chopped

2 garlic cloves, finely chopped

1 1/2 tbsp chopped fresh thyme leaves

2 bay leaves

2 red bell peppers, seeded and coarsely chopped

1 lb 12 oz/800 g canned chopped tomatoes

1 tsp smoked paprika

1 cup fish stock

1 cup blanched almonds, toasted and finely ground

salt and pepper

12–16 live mussels

12–16 live clams

1 lb 5 oz/600 g thick boned hake or cod fillets, skinned and cut into 2-inch/5-cm chunks

12–16 raw shrimp, shelled and deveined

thick crusty bread, to serve

Seafood Hotpot with Red Wine & Tomatoes

Remove the beards from the mussels. Rinse the mussels well, and discard any with broken shells or any that refuse to close when tapped.

Heat the oil in a large, heavy pan or flameproof casserole over medium heat. Add the onion and bell pepper. Cook for 5 minutes, or until beginning to soften. Stir in the garlic, tomato paste, parsley, and oregano. Cook for 1 minute, stirring. Pour in the tomatoes and wine. Season to taste with salt and pepper. Bring to a boil, then cover, and simmer over low heat for 30 minutes. Add the fish. Cover and simmer for 15 minutes.

Add the mussels, scallops, shrimp, and crabmeat. Cover and cook for 15 minutes more. Discard any mussels that have not opened. Stir in the basil just before serving.

SERVES 4–6

12 oz/350 g mussels, scrubbed

4 tbsp olive oil

1 onion, finely chopped

1 green bell pepper, seeded and chopped

2 garlic cloves, very finely chopped

5 tbsp tomato paste

1 tbsp chopped fresh flat-leaf parsley

1 tsp dried oregano

14 oz/400 g canned chopped tomatoes

1 cup dry red wine

salt and pepper

1 lb/450 g firm white fish, such as cod or monkfish, cut into 2-inch/5-cm pieces

4 oz/115 g scallops, halved

1 cup peeled raw shrimp

7 oz/200 g canned crabmeat

10–15 fresh basil leaves, shredded, to garnish

Squid with Parsley & Pine Nuts

Place the golden raisins in a small bowl, cover with lukewarm water, and set aside for 15 minutes to plump up.

Meanwhile, heat the olive oil in a heavy-bottom pan. Add the parsley and garlic and cook over low heat, stirring frequently, for 3 minutes. Add the squid and cook, stirring occasionally, for 5 minutes.

Increase the heat to medium, pour in the wine, and cook until it has almost completely evaporated. Stir in the strained tomatoes and season to taste with chili powder and salt. Reduce the heat again, cover, and let simmer gently, stirring occasionally, for 45–50 minutes, until the squid is almost tender.

Drain the golden raisins and stir them into the pan with the pine nuts. Let simmer for an additional 10 minutes, then serve immediately garnished with the reserved chopped parsley.

SERVES 4

$1/2$ cup golden raisins

5 tbsp olive oil

2 tbsp chopped fresh flat-leaf parsley, plus extra to garnish

2 garlic cloves, finely chopped

1 lb 12 oz/800 g prepared squid, sliced, or squid rings

$1/2$ cup dry white wine

1 lb 2 oz/500 g strained tomatoes

pinch of chili powder

salt

$3/4$ cup pine nuts, finely chopped

Seafood in Saffron Sauce

Clean the mussels and clams by scrubbing or scraping the shells and pulling out any beards that are attached to the mussels. Discard any with broken shells or any that refuse to close when tapped.

Heat the oil in a large, flameproof casserole and cook the onion with the saffron, thyme, and a pinch of salt over low heat, stirring occasionally, for 5 minutes, or until softened.

Add the garlic and cook, stirring, for 2 minutes. Add the tomatoes, wine, and stock, then season to taste with salt and pepper and stir well. Bring to a boil, then reduce the heat and simmer for 15 minutes.

Add the fish chunks and simmer for an additional 3 minutes. Add the clams, mussels, and squid rings and simmer for an additional 5 minutes, or until the mussels and clams have opened. Discard any that remain closed. Stir in the basil and serve immediately, accompanied by plenty of fresh bread to mop up the broth.

SERVES 4

8 oz/225 g live mussels

8 oz/225 g live clams

2 tbsp olive oil

1 onion, sliced

pinch of saffron threads

1 tbsp chopped fresh thyme

salt and pepper

2 garlic cloves, finely chopped

1 lb 12 oz/800 g canned tomatoes, drained and chopped

$^3/_4$ cup dry white wine

8 cups fish stock

12 oz/350 g red snapper fillets, cut into bite-size chunks

1 lb/450 g monkfish fillet, cut into bite-size chunks

8 oz/225 g raw squid rings

2 tbsp fresh shredded basil leaves

fresh bread, to serve

Moroccan Fish Tagine

Heat the olive oil in a flameproof casserole. Add the onion and cook gently over very low heat, stirring occasionally, for 10 minutes, or until softened, but not colored. Add the saffron, ground cinnamon, coriander, cumin, and turmeric and cook for an additional 30 seconds, stirring constantly.

Add the tomatoes and fish stock and stir well. Bring to a boil, reduce the heat, cover, and simmer for 15 minutes. Uncover and simmer for 20–35 minutes, or until thickened.

Cut each red snapper in half, then add the fish pieces to the casserole, pushing them down into the liquid. Simmer the stew for an additional 5–6 minutes, or until the fish is just cooked.

Carefully stir in the olives, lemon, and fresh cilantro. Season to taste with salt and pepper and serve immediately with couscous.

SERVES 4

2 tbsp olive oil

1 large onion, finely chopped

pinch of saffron threads

$1/2$ tsp ground cinnamon

1 tsp ground coriander

$1/2$ tsp ground cumin

$1/2$ tsp ground turmeric

7 oz/200 g canned chopped
   tomatoes

$1^1/_4$ cups fish stock

4 small red snappers, cleaned,
   boned, and heads and tails
   removed

2 oz/55 g pitted green olives

1 tbsp chopped preserved lemon

3 tbsp chopped fresh cilantro

salt and pepper

freshly cooked couscous, to serve

Seafood Chili

Place the shrimp, scallops, monkfish chunks, and lime slices in a large, nonmetallic dish with 1/4 teaspoon of the chili powder, 1/4 teaspoon of the ground cumin, 1 tablespoon of the chopped cilantro, half the garlic, the fresh chile, and 1 tablespoon of the oil. Cover with plastic wrap and let marinate for up to 1 hour.

Meanwhile, heat 1 tablespoon of the remaining oil in a flameproof casserole or large, heavy-bottom pan. Add the onion, the remaining garlic, and the red and yellow bell peppers and cook over low heat, stirring occasionally, for 5 minutes, or until softened. Add the remaining chili powder, the remaining cumin, the cloves, cinnamon, and cayenne with the remaining oil, if necessary, and season to taste with salt. Cook, stirring, for 5 minutes, then gradually stir in the stock and the tomatoes and their juices. Partially cover and simmer for 25 minutes.

Add the beans to the tomato mixture and spoon the fish and shellfish on top. Cover and cook for 10 minutes, or until the fish and shellfish are cooked through. Sprinkle with the remaining cilantro and serve.

SERVES 4

4 oz/115 g raw shrimp, peeled

9 oz/250 g prepared scallops, thawed if frozen

4 oz/115 g monkfish fillet, cut into chunks

1 lime, peeled and thinly sliced

1 tbsp chili powder

1 tsp ground cumin

3 tbsp chopped fresh cilantro

2 garlic cloves, finely chopped

1 fresh green chile, seeded and chopped

3 tbsp corn oil

1 onion, coarsely chopped

1 red bell pepper, seeded and coarsely chopped

1 yellow bell pepper, seeded and coarsely chopped

1/4 tsp ground cloves

pinch of ground cinnamon

pinch of cayenne pepper

salt

1 1/2 cups fish stock

14 oz/400 g canned chopped tomatoes

14 oz/400 g canned red kidney beans, drained and rinsed

Mediterranean Fish Stew

Heat the oil in a large, flameproof casserole. Add the onion, saffron, thyme, and a pinch of salt. Cook over low heat, stirring occasionally, for 5 minutes, or until the onion has softened.

Add the garlic and cook for an additional 2 minutes, then add the drained tomatoes and pour in the stock and wine. Season to taste with salt and pepper, bring the mixture to a boil, then reduce the heat and simmer for 15 minutes.

Add the chunks of red snapper and monkfish and simmer for 3 minutes. Add the clams and squid and simmer for 5 minutes, or until the clam shells have opened. Discard any clams that remain closed. Tear in the basil and stir. Serve garnished with the extra basil leaves.

SERVES 4

2 tbsp olive oil

1 onion, sliced

pinch of saffron threads, lightly crushed

1 tbsp chopped fresh thyme

salt and pepper

2 garlic cloves, finely chopped

1 lb 12 oz/800 g canned chopped tomatoes, drained

8 cups fish stock

$^3/_4$ cup dry white wine

12 oz/350 g red snapper or pompano fillets, cut into chunks

1 lb/450 g monkfish fillet, cut into chunks

1 lb/450 g fresh clams, scrubbed

8 oz/225 g squid rings

2 tbsp fresh basil leaves, plus extra to garnish

Italian Fish Stew

Heat the oil in a large pan. Add the onions and garlic and cook over low heat, stirring occasionally, for about 5 minutes until softened. Add the zucchini and cook, stirring frequently, for 2–3 minutes.

Add the tomatoes and stock to the pan and bring to a boil. Add the pasta, bring back to a boil, reduce the heat, and cover. Simmer for 5 minutes.

Skin and bone the fish, then cut it into chunks. Add to the pan with the basil or oregano and lemon rind and simmer gently for 5 minutes until the fish is opaque and flakes easily (take care not to overcook it) and the pasta is tender, but still firm to the bite.

Blend the cornstarch with the water to a smooth paste and stir into the stew. Cook gently for 2 minutes, stirring constantly, until thickened. Season with salt and pepper to taste.

Ladle the stew into 4 warmed bowls. Garnish with basil or oregano and serve immediately.

SERVES 4

2 tbsp olive oil

2 red onions, finely chopped

1 garlic clove, crushed

2 zucchini, sliced

14 oz/400 g canned chopped tomatoes

$3^3/_4$ cups fish or vegetable stock

$^3/_4$ cup dried pasta shapes

12 oz/350 g firm white fish, such as cod, haddock, or hake

1 tbsp chopped fresh basil or oregano or 1 tsp dried oregano

1 tsp grated lemon rind

1 tbsp cornstarch

1 tbsp water

salt and pepper

chopped fresh basil or oregano, to garnish

Moules Marinières

Clean the mussels by scrubbing or scraping the shells and pulling off any beards. Discard any with broken shells or any that refuse to close when tapped with a knife. Rinse the mussels under cold running water.

Pour the wine into a large, heavy-bottom pan, add the shallots and bouquet garni, and season to taste with pepper. Bring to a boil over medium heat. Add the mussels, cover tightly, and cook, shaking the pan occasionally, for 5 minutes. Remove and discard the bouquet garni and any mussels that remain closed. Divide the mussels among 4 soup plates with a slotted spoon. Tilt the casserole to let any sand settle, then spoon the cooking liquid over the mussels and serve immediately with bread.

SERVES 4

4 lb 8 oz/2 kg live mussels

1 1/4 cups dry white wine

6 shallots, finely chopped

1 bouquet garni

pepper

crusty bread, to serve

Roasted Seafood

Preheat the oven to 400°F/200°C. Scrub the potatoes to remove any dirt. Cut any large potatoes in half. Parboil the potatoes in a pan of boiling water for 10–15 minutes.

Place the potatoes in a large roasting pan together with the onions, zucchini, garlic, lemons, and rosemary sprigs.

Pour over the oil and toss to coat all the vegetables in it. Roast in the oven for 30 minutes, turning occasionally, until the potatoes are tender.

Once the potatoes are tender, add the shrimp, squid, and tomatoes, tossing to coat them in the oil, and roast for 5 minutes. All the vegetables should be cooked through and slightly charred for full flavor.

Transfer the roasted seafood and vegetables to warmed serving plates and serve hot.

SERVES 4

1 lb 5 oz/600 g new potatoes

3 red onions, cut into wedges

2 zucchini, cut into chunks

8 garlic cloves, peeled but left whole

2 lemons, cut into wedges

4 fresh rosemary sprigs

4 tbsp olive oil

12 oz/350 g unshelled raw shrimp

2 small raw squid, cut into rings

4 tomatoes, quartered

Goan-Style Seafood Curry

Heat the oil in a kadhai, wok, or large skillet over high heat. Add the mustard seeds and stir them around for about 1 minute, or until they jump. Stir in the curry leaves.

Add the shallots and garlic and stir for about 5 minutes, or until the shallots are golden. Stir in the turmeric, coriander, and chili powder and continue stirring for about 30 seconds.

Add the dissolved creamed coconut. Bring to a boil, then reduce the heat to medium and stir for about 2 minutes.

Reduce the heat to low, add the fish, and simmer for 1 minute, spooning the sauce over the fish and very gently stirring it around. Add the shrimp and continue to simmer for an additional 4–5 minutes until the fish flesh flakes easily and the shrimp turn pink and curl.

Add half the lime juice, then taste and add more lime juice and salt to taste. Sprinkle with the lime rind and serve with lime wedges.

SERVES 4–6

3 tbsp vegetable or peanut oil

1 tbsp black mustard seeds

12 fresh curry leaves or 1 tbsp dried

6 shallots, finely chopped

1 garlic clove, crushed

1 tsp ground turmeric

$1/2$ tsp ground coriander

$1/4$–$1/2$ tsp chili powder

5 oz/140 g creamed coconut, grated and dissolved in $1^1/4$ cups boiling water

1 lb 2 oz/500 g skinless, boneless white fish, such as monkfish or cod, cut into large chunks

1 lb/450 g large raw shrimp, shelled and deveined

juice and finely grated rind of 1 lime

salt

lime wedges, to serve

Jambalaya

Heat the vegetable oil in a large skillet over low heat. Add the onions, bell pepper, celery, and garlic and cook for 8–10 minutes until all the vegetables have softened. Add the paprika and cook for another 30 seconds. Add the chicken and sausages and cook for 8–10 minutes until lightly browned. Add the tomatoes and cook for 2–3 minutes until they have collapsed.

Add the rice to the pan and stir well. Pour in the hot stock, oregano, and bay leaves and stir well. Cover and let simmer for 10 minutes.

Add the shrimp and stir well. Cover again and cook for another 6–8 minutes until the rice is tender and the shrimp are cooked through.

Stir in the scallions and parsley, and season to taste with salt and pepper. Transfer to a large serving dish, garnish with chopped fresh herbs and serve.

SERVES 4

2 tbsp vegetable oil

2 onions, coarsely chopped

1 green bell pepper, seeded and coarsely chopped

2 celery stalks, coarsely chopped

3 garlic cloves, finely chopped

2 tsp paprika

$10\frac{1}{2}$ oz/300 g skinless, boneless chicken breasts, chopped

$3\frac{1}{2}$ oz/100 g boudin sausages, chopped

3 tomatoes, peeled and chopped

2 cups long-grain rice

$3\frac{3}{4}$ cups hot chicken or fish stock

1 tsp dried oregano

2 bay leaves

12 large jumbo shrimp

4 scallions, finely chopped

2 tbsp chopped fresh parsley

salt and pepper

chopped fresh herbs, to garnish

Shrimp with Coconut Rice

Place the mushrooms in a small bowl, cover with hot water, and set aside to soak for 30 minutes. Drain, then cut off and discard the stalks and slice the caps.

Heat 1 tablespoon of the oil in a wok and stir-fry the scallions, coconut, and chile for 2–3 minutes, until lightly browned. Add the mushrooms and stir-fry for 3–4 minutes.

Add the rice and stir-fry for 2–3 minutes, then add the stock and bring to a boil. Reduce the heat and add the coconut milk. Let simmer for 10–15 minutes, until the rice is tender. Stir in the shrimp and basil, heat through, and serve.

SERVES 4

1 cup dried Chinese mushrooms

2 tbsp vegetable or peanut oil

6 scallions, chopped

scant $^1/_2$ cup dry unsweetened coconut

1 fresh green chile, seeded and chopped

generous 1 cup jasmine rice

$^2/_3$ cup fish stock

1$^3/_4$ cups coconut milk

12 oz/350 g cooked shelled shrimp

6 sprigs fresh Thai basil

Shrimp Biryani

Soak the saffron in the lukewarm water for 10 minutes. Put the shallots, garlic, spices, chile, and salt into a spice grinder and grind to a paste or use a mortar and pestle.

Heat the ghee in a saucepan and add the mustard seeds. When they start to pop, add the shrimp and stir over a high heat for 1 minute. Stir in the spice mix, then the coconut milk and yogurt. Simmer for 20 minutes.

Spoon the shrimp mixture into serving bowls. Top with the freshly cooked basmati rice and drizzle over the saffron water. Serve, garnished with the almonds, scallion, and sprigs of cilantro.

SERVES 8

1 tsp saffron strands

4 tbsp lukewarm water

2 shallots, coarsely chopped

3 garlic cloves, crushed

1 tsp chopped gingerroot

2 tsp coriander seeds

$^1/_2$ tsp black peppercorns

2 cloves

seeds from 2 green cardamom pods

1-inch/2.5-cm piece cinnamon stick

1 tsp ground turmeric

1 fresh green chile, chopped

$^1/_2$ tsp salt

2 tbsp ghee

1 tsp whole black mustard seeds

1 lb 2 oz/500 g raw jumbo shrimp
  in their shells, or 14 oz/400 g raw
  and peeled

1$^1/_4$ cups coconut milk

1$^1/_4$ cups lowfat plain yogurt

freshly cooked basmati rice,
  to serve

to garnish

slivered almonds, toasted

1 scallion, sliced

sprigs of fresh cilantro

Shrimp & Chicken Paella

Soak the mussels in lightly salted water for 10 minutes. Put the saffron threads and water in a small bowl or cup and let infuse for a few minutes. Meanwhile, put the rice in a strainer and rinse in cold water until the water runs clear. Set aside.

Clean the mussels by scrubbing the shells and pulling out any beards that are attached to them. Discard any with broken shells or any that refuse to close when tapped. Set aside.

Heat 3 tablespoons of the oil in a 12-inch/30-cm paella pan or ovenproof casserole. Cook the chicken thighs over medium-high heat, turning frequently, for 5 minutes, or until golden and crispy. Using a slotted spoon, transfer to a bowl. Add the chorizo to the pan and cook, stirring, for 1 minute, or until beginning to crisp. Add to the chicken.

Heat the remaining oil in the pan and cook the onions, stirring frequently, for 2 minutes, then add the garlic and paprika and cook for an additional 3 minutes, or until the onions are soft but not browned.

Add the drained rice, beans, and peas and stir until coated in oil. Return the chicken and chorizo and any accumulated juices to the pan. Stir in the stock, saffron and its soaking liquid, and salt and pepper to taste and bring to a boil, stirring constantly. Reduce the heat to low and let simmer, uncovered and without stirring, for 15 minutes, or until the rice is almost tender and most of the liquid has been absorbed.

Arrange the mussels, shrimp, and red bell peppers on top, then cover and simmer, without stirring, for an additional 5 minutes, or until the shrimp turn pink and the mussels open. Discard any mussels that remain closed. Taste and adjust the seasoning if necessary. Sprinkle with the parsley and serve immediately.

SERVES 6–8

16 live mussels

$1/2$ tsp saffron threads

2 tbsp hot water

generous $1^3/4$ cups medium-grain paella rice

6 tbsp olive oil

6–8 unboned, skin-on chicken thighs, excess fat removed

5 oz/140 g Spanish chorizo sausage, casing removed, cut into $1/4$-inch/ 5-mm slices

2 large onions, chopped

4 large garlic cloves, crushed

1 tsp mild or hot Spanish paprika, to taste

$3^1/2$ oz/100 g green beans, chopped

generous $3/4$ cup frozen peas

5 cups fish, chicken, or vegetable stock

salt and pepper

16 raw shrimp, shelled and deveined

2 red bell peppers, halved and seeded, then broiled, peeled, and sliced

$1^1/4$ oz/35 g fresh chopped parsley, to garnish

Seafood Risotto

Heat the oil with 2 tablespoons of the butter in a deep pan over medium heat until the butter has melted. Add the garlic and cook, stirring, for 1 minute.

Reduce the heat, add the rice, and mix to coat in oil and butter. Cook, stirring constantly, for 2–3 minutes, or until the grains are translucent.

Gradually add the hot stock, a ladleful at a time. Stir constantly and add more liquid as the rice absorbs each addition. Increase the heat to medium so that the liquid bubbles. Cook for 20 minutes, or until all the liquid is absorbed and the rice is creamy. About 5 minutes before the rice is ready, add the seafood and oregano to the pan and mix well.

Remove the pan from the heat and season to taste. Add the remaining butter and mix well, then stir in the grated cheese until it melts. Spoon onto warmed plates and serve at once, garnished with extra oregano.

SERVES 4

1 tbsp olive oil

2 oz/55 g butter

2 garlic cloves, chopped

$1^3/_4$ cups risotto rice

generous $5^1/_2$ cups boiling fish or chicken stock

9 oz/250 g mixed cooked seafood, such as shrimp, squid, mussels, and clams

2 tbsp chopped fresh oregano, plus extra to garnish

salt and pepper

$^1/_2$ cup freshly grated romano or Parmesan cheese

Spicy Tuna with Fennel & Onion

Whisk all the marinade ingredients together in a small bowl. Put the tuna steaks in a large, shallow dish and spoon over 4 tablespoons of the marinade, turning until well coated. Cover and let marinate in the refrigerator for 30 minutes. Set aside the remaining marinade.

Heat a stovetop ridged grill pan over high heat. Put the fennel and onions in a separate bowl, add the oil, and toss well to coat. Add to the grill pan and cook for 5 minutes on each side until just beginning to color. Transfer to 4 warmed serving plates, drizzle with the reserved marinade, and keep warm.

Add the tuna steaks to the grill pan and cook, turning once, for 4–5 minutes until firm to the touch but still moist inside. Transfer the tuna to the serving plates and serve at once with crusty rolls.

SERVES 4

4 tuna steaks, about 5 oz/ 140 g each
2 fennel bulbs, thickly sliced lengthwise
2 red onions, sliced
2 tbsp extra-virgin olive oil
crusty rolls, to serve

for the marinade

$1/2$ cup extra-virgin olive oil
4 garlic cloves, finely chopped
4 fresh red chiles, seeded and finely chopped
juice and finely grated rind of 2 lemons
4 tbsp finely chopped fresh flat-leaf parsley
salt and pepper

Swordfish with Tomatoes & Olives

Heat the oil in a large, heavy-bottom pan. Add the onion and celery and cook over low heat, stirring occasionally, for 5 minutes, or until softened.

Meanwhile, roughly chop half the olives. Stir the chopped and whole olives into the pan with the tomatoes and capers and season to taste with salt and pepper.

Bring to a boil, then reduce the heat, cover, and simmer gently, stirring occasionally, for 15 minutes.

Add the swordfish steaks to the pan and return to a boil. Cover and simmer, turning the fish once, for 20 minutes, or until the fish is cooked and the flesh flakes easily. Transfer the fish to serving plates and spoon the sauce over them. Garnish with parsley and serve immediately.

SERVES 4

2 tbsp olive oil

1 onion, finely chopped

1 celery stalk, finely chopped

4 oz/115 g green olives, pitted

1 lb/450 g tomatoes, chopped

3 tbsp bottled capers, drained

salt and pepper

4 swordfish steaks, about
   5 oz/140 g each

fresh flat-leaf parsley sprigs,
   to garnish

Spicy Monkfish Rice

In a food processor or blender, blend the fresh and dried chile, garlic, saffron, mint, olive oil, and lemon juice until finely chopped but not smooth.

Put the monkfish into a nonmetallic dish and pour over the spice paste, mixing together well. Set aside for 20 minutes to marinate.

Heat a large pan until it is very hot. Using a slotted spoon, lift the monkfish from the marinade and add, in batches, to the hot pan. Cook for 3–4 minutes until browned and firm. Remove with a slotted spoon and set aside while you cook the rice.

Add the onion and remaining marinade to the same pan and cook for 5 minutes until softened and lightly browned. Add the rice and stir until well coated. Add the tomatoes and coconut milk. Bring to a boil, cover, and simmer very gently for 15 minutes. Stir in the peas, season, and arrange the fish over the top. Cover with foil and continue to cook over very low heat for 5 minutes. Serve garnished with the chopped mint.

SERVES 4

1 hot red chile, seeded and chopped

1 tsp chile flakes

2 garlic cloves, chopped

2 pinches of saffron

3 tbsp coarsely chopped mint leaves

4 tbsp olive oil

2 tbsp lemon juice

12 oz/350 g monkfish fillet, cut into bite-sized pieces

1 onion, finely chopped

1 cup long-grain rice

14 oz/400 g canned chopped tomatoes

$^3/_4$ cup coconut milk

1 cup peas

salt and pepper

2 tbsp chopped fresh mint, to garnish

Monkfish Packages

Preheat the oven to 375°F/190°C. Cut 4 large pieces of foil, about 9-inches/23-cm square. Brush lightly with a little of the oil, then divide the zucchini and bell pepper among them.

Rinse the fish fillets under cold running water and pat dry with paper towels. Cut them in half, then put 1 piece on top of each pile of zucchini and bell pepper. Cut the bacon slices in half and lay 3 pieces across each piece of fish. Season to taste with salt and pepper, drizzle over the remaining oil, and close up the packages. Seal tightly, transfer to an ovenproof dish, and bake in the preheated oven for 25 minutes.

Remove from the oven, open each foil package slightly, and serve with pasta and slices of olive bread.

SERVES 4

4 tsp olive oil

2 zucchini, sliced

1 large red bell pepper, peeled, seeded, and cut into strips

2 monkfish fillets, about 4½ oz/125 g each, skin and membrane removed

6 smoked lean bacon slices

salt and pepper

to serve

freshly cooked pasta

slices of olive bread

Roasted Monkfish

Preheat the oven to 400°F/200°C. Remove the central bone from the fish if not already removed and make small slits down each fillet. Cut 2 of the garlic cloves into thin slivers and insert into the fish. Place the fish on a sheet of waxed paper, season with salt and pepper to taste, and drizzle over 1 tablespoon of the oil. Bring the top edges together. Form into a pleat and fold over, then fold the ends underneath, completely encasing the fish. Set aside.

Put the remaining garlic cloves and all the vegetables into a roasting pan and drizzle with the remaining oil, turning the vegetables so that they are well coated in the oil.

Roast in the preheated oven for 20 minutes, turning occasionally. Put the fish package on top of the vegetables and cook for an additional 15–20 minutes, or until the vegetables are tender and the fish is cooked.

Remove from the oven and open up the package. Cut the monkfish into thick slices. Arrange the vegetables on warmed serving plates, top with the fish slices, and sprinkle with the basil. Serve at once.

SERVES 4

1 lb 8 oz/675 g monkfish tail, skinned

4–5 large garlic cloves, peeled

salt and pepper

3 tbsp olive oil

1 onion, cut into wedges

1 small eggplant, about 10½ oz/ 300 g, cut into chunks

1 red bell pepper, seeded, cut into wedges

1 yellow bell pepper, seeded, cut into wedges

1 large zucchini, about 8 oz/225 g, cut into wedges

1 tbsp shredded fresh basil

5

Vegetable Heaven

Eating plenty of healthy vegetables every day could not be easier or more fun than with this superb collection of international recipes. Whether your taste is for a medley of summer flavors, a spicy curry, a hearty winter warmer, a flavorsome gratin, or an elegant risotto, these delicious and easy-to-prepare vegetable dishes are sure to fill the bill. Economical, irresistible, nourishing, and all in a single pot—what more could anyone want?

Italian Vegetable Stew

Finely chop the garlic and dice the squash. Put them in a large, heavy-bottom pan with a tight-fitting lid. Add the onion, leeks, eggplant, celery root, turnips, tomatoes, carrot, zucchini, red bell peppers, fennel, Swiss chard, bay leaves, fennel seeds, chili powder, thyme, oregano, sugar, oil, stock, and half the basil to the pan. Mix together well, then bring to a boil.

Reduce the heat, then cover and simmer for 30 minutes, or until all the vegetables are tender.

Sprinkle in the remaining basil and the parsley and season to taste with salt and pepper. Serve immediately, sprinkled with the cheese.

SERVES 4

4 garlic cloves

1 small acorn squash, seeded and peeled

1 red onion, sliced

2 leeks, sliced

1 eggplant, sliced

1 small celery root, diced

2 turnips, sliced

2 plum tomatoes, chopped

1 carrot, sliced

1 zucchini, sliced

2 red bell peppers, seeded and chopped

1 fennel bulb, sliced

6 oz/175 g Swiss chard, chopped

2 bay leaves

$1/2$ tsp fennel seeds

$1/2$ tsp chili powder

pinch each of dried thyme, dried oregano, and sugar

$1/2$ cup extra-virgin olive oil

scant 1 cup vegetable stock

1 oz/25 g fresh basil leaves, torn

4 tbsp chopped fresh parsley

salt and pepper

2 tbsp freshly grated Parmesan cheese, to serve

Spring Stew

Heat the oil in a large, heavy-bottom pan with a tight-fitting lid, and cook the onions, celery, carrots, and potatoes, stirring frequently, for 5 minutes, or until softened. Add the stock, drained beans, bouquet garni, and soy sauce, then bring to a boil. Reduce the heat, then cover and simmer for 12 minutes.

Add the baby corn and fava beans and season to taste with salt and pepper. Simmer for an additional 3 minutes.

Meanwhile, discard the outer leaves and hard central core from the cabbage and shred the leaves. Add to the pan and simmer for an additional 3–5 minutes, or until all the vegetables are tender.

Blend the cornstarch with the water, then stir into the pan and cook, stirring, for 4–6 minutes, or until the liquid has thickened. Serve the cheese separately, for stirring into the stew.

SERVES 4

2 tbsp olive oil

4–8 baby onions, halved

2 celery stalks, cut into $^1/_4$-inch/ 5-mm slices

8 oz/225 g baby carrots, scrubbed and halved if large

$10^1/_2$ oz/300 g new potatoes, scrubbed and halved, or cut into quarters if large

$3^3/_4$–5 cups vegetable stock

generous $2^3/_4$ cups canned cannellini beans, drained and rinsed

1 fresh bouquet garni

$1^1/_2$–2 tbsp light soy sauce

3 oz/85 g baby corn

1 cup frozen or shelled fresh fava beans, thawed if frozen

salt and pepper

$^1/_2$–1 head of Savoy or spring cabbage, about 8 oz/225 g

$1^1/_2$ tbsp cornstarch

2 tbsp cold water

2–3 oz/55–85 g Parmesan or sharp Cheddar cheese, grated, to serve

Tuscan Bean Stew

Trim the fennel and reserve any feathery fronds, then cut the bulb into small strips. Heat the oil in a large, heavy-bottom pan with a tight-fitting lid, and cook the onion, garlic, chile, and fennel strips, stirring frequently, for 5–8 minutes, or until softened.

Add the eggplant and cook, stirring frequently, for 5 minutes. Blend the tomato paste with a little of the stock in a pitcher and pour over the fennel mixture, then add the remaining stock, and the tomatoes, vinegar, and oregano. Bring to a boil, then reduce the heat and simmer, covered, for 15 minutes, or until the tomatoes have begun to collapse.

Drain and rinse the beans, then drain again. Add them to the pan with the yellow bell pepper, zucchini, and olives. Simmer for an additional 15 minutes, or until the vegetables are tender. Taste and adjust the seasoning. Scatter with the Parmesan shavings and serve garnished with the reserved fennel fronds, accompanied by polenta wedges or crusty bread.

SERVES 4

1 large fennel bulb

2 tbsp olive oil

1 red onion, cut into small wedges

2–4 garlic cloves, sliced

1 fresh green chile, seeded and chopped

1 small eggplant, about 8 oz/225 g, cut into chunks

2 tbsp tomato paste

scant 2–2$\frac{1}{2}$ cups vegetable stock

1 lb/450 g ripe tomatoes

1 tbsp balsamic vinegar

a few sprigs of fresh oregano

14 oz/400 g canned cranberry beans

14 oz/400 g canned flageolets

1 yellow bell pepper, seeded and cut into small strips

1 zucchini, sliced into half moons

$\frac{1}{3}$ cup pitted black olives

salt and pepper

25 g/1 oz Parmesan cheese, freshly shaved

polenta wedges or crusty bread, to serve

Potato & Lemon Casserole

Heat the olive oil in a flameproof casserole. Add the onions and sauté over medium heat, stirring frequently, for 3 minutes.

Add the garlic and cook for 30 seconds. Stir in the ground cumin, ground coriander, and cayenne and cook, stirring constantly, for 1 minute.

Add the carrot, turnips, zucchini, and potatoes and stir to coat in the oil.

Add the lemon juice and rind and the vegetable stock. Season to taste with salt and pepper. Cover and cook over medium heat, stirring occasionally, for 20–30 minutes until tender.

Remove the lid, sprinkle in the chopped fresh cilantro and stir well. Serve immediately.

SERVES 4

scant $1/2$ cup olive oil

2 red onions, cut into 8 wedges

3 garlic cloves, crushed

2 tsp ground cumin

2 tsp ground coriander

pinch of cayenne pepper

1 carrot, thickly sliced

2 small turnips, quartered

1 zucchini, sliced

1 lb 2 oz/500 g potatoes, thickly sliced

juice and grated rind of 2 large lemons

$1^{1}/_{4}$ cups vegetable stock

salt and pepper

2 tbsp chopped fresh cilantro

Lentil & Rice Casserole

Place the lentils, rice, and vegetable stock in a large flameproof casserole and cook over low heat, stirring occasionally, for 20 minutes.

Add the leek, garlic, tomatoes and their can juice, ground cumin, chili powder, garam masala, sliced bell pepper, broccoli, baby corn, and green beans to the casserole.

Bring the mixture to a boil, reduce the heat, cover, and simmer for an additional 10–15 minutes or until all the vegetables are tender.

Add the shredded basil and season with salt and pepper to taste.

Garnish with fresh basil sprigs and serve immediately.

SERVES 4

1 cup red lentils

generous $\frac{1}{4}$ cup long-grain rice

5 cups vegetable stock

1 leek, cut into chunks

3 garlic cloves, crushed

14 oz/400 g canned chopped
   tomatoes

1 tsp ground cumin

1 tsp chili powder

1 tsp garam masala

1 red bell pepper, seeded and sliced

$3\frac{1}{2}$ oz/100 g small broccoli florets

8 baby corn, halved lengthwise

2 oz/55 g green beans, halved

1 tbsp shredded fresh basil

salt and pepper

fresh basil sprigs, to garnish

Vegetable Goulash

Put the sun-dried tomatoes in a small heatproof bowl, then cover with almost boiling water and let soak for 15–20 minutes. Drain, reserving the soaking liquid.

Heat the oil in a large, heavy-bottom pan, with a tight-fitting lid, and cook the chiles, garlic, and vegetables, stirring frequently, for 5–8 minutes, or until softened. Blend the tomato paste with a little of the stock in a pitcher and pour over the vegetable mixture, then add the remaining stock, lentils, the sun-dried tomatoes and their soaking liquid, and the paprika and thyme.

Bring to a boil, then reduce the heat and simmer, covered, for 15 minutes. Add the fresh tomatoes and simmer for an additional 15 minutes, or until the vegetables and lentils are tender. Serve topped with spoonfuls of sour cream, accompanied by crusty bread.

SERVES 4

$1/4$ cup sun-dried tomatoes, chopped

2 tbsp olive oil

$1/2$–1 tsp crushed dried chiles

2–3 garlic cloves, chopped

1 large onion, cut into small wedges

1 small celery root, cut into small chunks

8 oz/225 g carrots, sliced

8 oz/225 g new potatoes, scrubbed and cut into chunks

1 small acorn squash, seeded, peeled, and cut into small chunks, about 8 oz/225 g prepared weight

2 tbsp tomato paste

$1^1/4$ cups vegetable stock

$2^1/2$ cups canned Puy or green lentils, drained and rinsed

1–2 tsp hot paprika

few fresh sprigs of thyme

1 lb/450 g ripe tomatoes, coarsely chopped

to serve

sour cream

crusty bread

Moroccan Vegetable Stew

Heat the oil in a large, heavy-bottom pan with a tight-fitting lid, and cook the onion, garlic, chile, and eggplant, stirring frequently, for 5–8 minutes, or until softened.

Add the ginger, cumin, coriander, and saffron and cook, stirring constantly, for 2 minutes. Bruise the cinnamon stick.

Add the cinnamon, squash, sweet potatoes, prunes, stock, and tomatoes to the pan and bring to a boil. Reduce the heat, then cover and simmer, stirring occasionally, for 20 minutes. Add the chickpeas to the pan and cook for an additional 10 minutes. Discard the cinnamon and serve garnished with the fresh cilantro.

SERVES 4

2 tbsp olive oil

1 red onion, finely chopped

2–4 garlic cloves, crushed

1 fresh red chile, seeded and sliced

1 eggplant, about 8 oz/225 g, cut into small chunks

small piece fresh gingerroot, peeled and grated

1 tsp ground cumin

1 tsp ground coriander

pinch of saffron threads or $1/2$ tsp turmeric

1–2 cinnamon sticks

$1/2$–1 butternut squash, about 1 lb/450 g, peeled, seeded, and cut into small chunks

8 oz/225 g sweet potatoes, cut into small chunks

scant $1/2$ cup dried prunes

2–$2^{1}/_{2}$ cups vegetable stock

4 tomatoes, chopped

14 oz/400 g canned chickpeas, drained and rinsed

1 tbsp chopped fresh cilantro, to garnish

Chile Bean Stew

Heat the oil in a large, heavy-bottom pan with a tight-fitting lid, and cook the onion, garlic, and chiles, stirring frequently, for 5 minutes, or until softened. Add the kidney and cannellini beans and the chickpeas. Blend the tomato paste with a little of the stock in a pitcher and pour over the bean mixture, then add the remaining stock. Bring to a boil, then reduce the heat and simmer for 10–15 minutes.

Add the red bell pepper, tomatoes, fava beans, and pepper to taste and simmer for 15–20 minutes, or until all the vegetables are tender. Stir in the chopped cilantro.

Serve the stew topped with spoonfuls of sour cream and garnished with chopped cilantro and a pinch of paprika.

SERVES 4–6

2 tbsp olive oil

1 onion, chopped

2–4 garlic cloves, chopped

2 fresh red chiles, seeded and sliced

$1^2/_3$ cups canned kidney beans, drained and rinsed

$1^2/_3$ cups canned cannellini beans, drained and rinsed

$1^2/_3$ cups canned chickpeas, drained and rinsed

1 tbsp tomato paste

$3–3^3/_4$ cups vegetable stock

1 red bell pepper, seeded and chopped

4 tomatoes, coarsely chopped

$1^1/_2$ cups frozen or shelled fresh fava beans, thawed if frozen

pepper

1 tbsp chopped fresh cilantro

sour cream, to serve

to garnish

chopped fresh cilantro

pinch of paprika

Vegetable & Lentil Casserole

Preheat the oven to 350°F/180°C. Press the cloves into the onion. Put the lentils into a large casserole, then add the onion and bay leaf and pour in the stock. Cover and cook in the preheated oven for 1 hour.

Remove the onion and discard the cloves. Slice the onion and return it to the casserole with the vegetables. Stir thoroughly and season to taste with salt and pepper. Cover and return to the oven for 1 hour.

Discard the bay leaf. Stir in the lemon juice and serve straight from the casserole.

SERVES 4

10 cloves

1 onion, peeled but kept whole

$1^1/_8$ cups Puy or green lentils

1 bay leaf

$6^1/_4$ cups vegetable stock

salt and pepper

2 leeks, sliced

2 potatoes, diced

2 carrots, chopped

3 zucchini, sliced

1 celery stalk, chopped

1 red bell pepper, seeded and chopped

1 tbsp lemon juice

Vegetable Chili

Brush the eggplant slices on one side with 1 teaspoon of the olive oil. Heat 1 teaspoon of the oil in a large, heavy skillet over medium-high heat. Add the eggplant slices, oiled-side up, and cook for 5–6 minutes until browned on one side. Turn the slices over, cook on the other side until browned and then transfer to a plate. Cut the slices into bite-sized pieces.

Heat the remaining oil in a large pan over medium heat. Add the onion and bell peppers and cook, stirring occasionally, for 3–4 minutes until the onion is just softened, but not browned. Add the garlic and continue cooking for 2–3 minutes or until the onion is just beginning to color.

Add the tomatoes, chili powder, cumin, and oregano. Season to taste with salt and pepper. Bring just to a boil, reduce the heat, cover, and simmer gently for 15 minutes.

Add the zucchini, eggplant pieces, and kidney beans. Stir in the water and tomato paste. Bring back to a boil, cover, and continue simmering for about 45 minutes or until the vegetables are tender. Adjust the seasoning if necessary. If you prefer a hotter dish, stir in a little more chili powder.

Ladle into warmed bowls and top with scallions and cheese.

SERVES 4

1 medium eggplant, peeled if wished, cut into 1-inch/2.5-cm slices

4 tsp olive oil

1 large red or yellow onion, finely chopped

2 red or yellow bell peppers, seeded and finely chopped

3–4 garlic cloves, finely chopped or crushed

1 lb 12 oz/800 g canned chopped tomatoes

1 tbsp mild chili powder

$^1/_2$ tsp ground cumin

$^1/_2$ tsp dried oregano

salt and pepper

2 small zucchini, quartered lengthwise and sliced

14 oz/400 g canned kidney beans, drained and rinsed

2 cups water

1 tbsp tomato paste

6 scallions, finely chopped, to serve

1 cup grated Cheddar cheese, to serve

Roasted Summer Vegetables

Preheat the oven to 400°F/200°C. Brush an ovenproof dish with a little oil. Arrange the fennel, onions, tomatoes, eggplant, zucchini, and bell peppers in the dish and tuck the garlic cloves and rosemary sprigs among them. Drizzle with the remaining oil and season to taste with pepper.

Roast the vegetables in the preheated oven for 10 minutes.

Turn the vegetables over, return the dish to the oven, and roast for an additional 10–15 minutes, or until the vegetables are tender and beginning to turn golden brown.

Serve the vegetables straight from the dish or transfer to a warm serving platter. Serve immediately, with crusty bread, if you like, to soak up the juices.

SERVES 4

2 tbsp olive oil

1 fennel bulb, cut into wedges

2 red onions, cut into wedges

2 beefsteak tomatoes, cut into wedges

1 eggplant, thickly sliced

2 zucchini, thickly sliced

1 yellow bell pepper, seeded and cut into chunks

1 red bell pepper, seeded and cut into chunks

1 orange bell pepper, seeded and cut into chunks

4 garlic cloves

4 fresh rosemary sprigs

ground black pepper

crusty bread, to serve (optional)

Ratatouille

Roughly chop the eggplants and zucchini, and seed and chop the bell peppers. Slice the onions and finely chop the garlic. Heat the oil in a large pan. Add the onions and cook over low heat, stirring occasionally, for 5 minutes, or until softened. Add the garlic and cook, stirring frequently for an additional 2 minutes.

Add the eggplants, zucchini, and bell peppers. Increase the heat to medium and cook, stirring occasionally, until the bell peppers begin to color. Add the bouquet garni, reduce the heat, cover, and simmer gently for 40 minutes.

Stir in the chopped tomatoes and season to taste with salt and pepper. Re-cover the pan and simmer gently for an additional 10 minutes. Remove and discard the bouquet garni. Serve warm or cold.

SERVES 4

2 eggplants

4 zucchini

2 yellow bell peppers

2 red bell peppers

2 onions

2 garlic cloves

$^2/_3$ cup olive oil

1 bouquet garni

3 large tomatoes, peeled, seeded, and coarsely chopped

salt and pepper

Eggplant Gratin

Heat the oil in a flameproof casserole over medium heat. Add the onion and cook for 5 minutes, or until soft. Add the garlic and cook for a few seconds, or until just beginning to color. Using a slotted spoon, transfer the onion mixture to a plate.

Cook the eggplant slices in batches in the same flameproof casserole until they are just lightly browned. Transfer to another plate.

Preheat the oven to 400°F/200°C. Arrange a layer of eggplant slices in the bottom of the casserole dish or a shallow ovenproof dish. Sprinkle with the parsley, thyme, salt, and pepper.

Add a layer of onion, tomatoes, and mozzarella, sprinkling parsley, thyme, salt, and pepper over each layer.

Continue layering, finishing with a layer of eggplant slices. Sprinkle with the Parmesan. Bake, uncovered, for 20–30 minutes, or until the top is golden and the eggplants are tender. Serve hot.

SERVES 2

4 tbsp olive oil

2 onions, finely chopped

2 garlic cloves, very finely chopped

2 eggplants, thickly sliced

3 tbsp fresh flat-leaf parsley, chopped

$^1/_2$ tsp dried thyme

salt and pepper

14 oz/400 g canned chopped tomatoes

1$^1/_2$ cups coarsely grated mozzarella

6 tbsp freshly grated Parmesan

Vegetable Curry

Cut the eggplant, turnips, and potatoes into $^1/_2$-inch/1-cm cubes. Divide the cauliflower into small florets. The button mushrooms can be used whole or sliced thickly, if preferred. Slice the onion and carrots.

Heat the ghee in a large pan. Add the onion, turnips, potatoes, and cauliflower and cook over low heat, stirring frequently, for 3 minutes. Add the garlic, gingerroot, chiles, paprika, ground coriander, and curry powder and cook, stirring, for 1 minute.

Add the stock, tomatoes, eggplant, and mushrooms and season with salt. Cover and simmer, stirring occasionally, for 30 minutes, or until tender. Add the green bell pepper and carrots, cover, and cook for an additional 5 minutes.

Place the cornstarch and coconut milk in a bowl, mix into a smooth paste, and stir into the vegetable mixture. Add the ground almonds and simmer, stirring constantly, for 2 minutes. Taste and adjust the seasoning, if necessary. Transfer to serving plates, garnish with cilantro sprigs, and serve immediately with freshly cooked rice.

SERVES 4

1 eggplant

8 oz/225 g turnips

12 oz/350 g new potatoes

8 oz/225 g cauliflower

8 oz/225 g button mushrooms

1 large onion

3 carrots

6 tbsp ghee

2 garlic cloves, crushed

4 tsp finely chopped fresh
   gingerroot

1–2 fresh green chiles, seeded
   and chopped

1 tbsp paprika

2 tsp ground coriander

1 tbsp mild or medium curry
   powder

scant 2 cups vegetable stock

14 oz/400 g canned chopped
   tomatoes

salt

1 green bell pepper, seeded and
   sliced

1 tbsp cornstarch

$^2/_3$ cup coconut milk

2–3 tbsp ground almonds

fresh cilantro sprigs, to garnish

freshly cooked rice, to serve

Cauliflower & Sweet Potato Curry

Heat the ghee in a large, heavy-bottom skillet. Add the onions and Bengali five-spice mix and cook over low heat, stirring frequently, for 10 minutes, or until the onions are golden. Add the cauliflower, sweet potatoes, and chiles and cook, stirring frequently, for 3 minutes.

Stir in the ginger paste, paprika, cumin, turmeric, and chili powder and cook, stirring constantly, for 3 minutes. Add the tomatoes and peas and stir in the yogurt and stock. Season with salt to taste, cover, and let simmer for 20 minutes, or until the vegetables are tender.

Sprinkle the garam masala over the curry, transfer to a warmed serving dish and serve immediately, garnished with sprigs of cilantro.

SERVES 4

4 tbsp ghee or vegetable oil

2 onions, finely chopped

1 tsp Bengali five-spice mix

1 head of cauliflower, broken into florets

12 oz/350 g sweet potatoes, diced

2 fresh green chiles, seeded and finely chopped

1 tsp ginger paste

2 tsp paprika

$1^1/_2$ tsp ground cumin

1 tsp ground turmeric

$^1/_2$ tsp chili powder

3 tomatoes, quartered

2 cups fresh or frozen peas

3 tbsp plain yogurt

1 cup vegetable stock or water

salt

1 tsp garam masala

sprigs of fresh cilantro, to garnish

Thai Red Curry with Cashews

To make the curry paste, place all the ingredients in a large mortar and pound with a pestle. Alternatively, process briefly in a food processor. (The quantity of red curry paste is more than is required for this recipe. Store for up to 3 weeks in a sealed jar in the refrigerator.)

Put a wok or heavy-based skillet over high heat, add 3 tablespoons of the red curry paste, and stir until it gives off its aroma. Reduce the heat to medium.

Add the coconut milk, kaffir lime leaf, light soy sauce, baby corn, broccoli florets, green beans, and cashew nuts. Bring to a boil and simmer for about 10 minutes until the vegetables are cooked, but still firm and crunchy.

Remove and discard the lime leaf and stir in the basil leaves and cilantro. Transfer to a warmed serving dish, garnish with peanuts, and serve.

SERVES 4

generous 1 cup coconut milk

1 kaffir lime leaf

$^1/_4$ tsp light soy sauce

4 baby corn, halved lengthwise

1 cup broccoli florets

$4^1/_2$ oz/125 g green beans, cut into 2-inch/5-cm pieces

4 tbsp cashew nuts

15 fresh basil leaves

1 tbsp chopped fresh cilantro

1 tbsp chopped roasted peanuts, to garnish

for the red curry paste

7 fresh red chiles, seeded and blanched

2 tsp cumin seeds

2 tsp coriander seeds

1-inch/2.5-cm piece galangal, chopped

$^1/_2$ lemongrass stalk, chopped

1 tsp salt

grated rind of 1 lime

4 garlic cloves, chopped

3 shallots, chopped

2 kaffir lime leaves, shredded

1 tbsp vegetable oil

Potato & Mushroom Bake

Preheat the oven to 375°F/190°C. Grease a shallow round ovenproof dish with butter.

Layer a quarter of the potatoes in the base of the dish. Arrange a quarter of the mushrooms on top of the potatoes and sprinkle with a quarter of the rosemary, chives, and garlic. Continue making layers in the same order, finishing with a layer of potatoes on top.

Pour the heavy cream over the top of the potatoes. Season to taste with salt and pepper.

Cook in the preheated oven for about 45 minutes, or until the bake is golden brown on top and piping hot.

Garnish with snipped chives and serve at once straight from the dish.

SERVES 4

2 tbsp butter

1 lb/450 g waxy potatoes, thinly sliced and parboiled

2 cups sliced mixed mushrooms

1 tbsp chopped rosemary

4 tbsp snipped chives, plus extra to garnish

2 garlic cloves, crushed

$^2/_3$ cup heavy cream

salt and pepper

Parmesan Cheese Risotto with Mushrooms

Heat the oil in a deep pan. Add the rice and cook over low heat, stirring constantly, for 2–3 minutes, until the grains are thoroughly coated in oil and translucent.

Add the garlic, onion, celery, and bell pepper and cook, stirring frequently, for 5 minutes. Add the mushrooms and cook for 3–4 minutes. Stir in the oregano.

Gradually add the hot stock, a ladleful at a time. Stir constantly and add more liquid as the rice absorbs each addition. Increase the heat to medium so that the liquid bubbles.

Cook for 20 minutes, or until all the liquid is absorbed and the rice is creamy. Add the sun-dried tomatoes, if using, 5 minutes before the end of the cooking time and season to taste with salt and pepper.

Remove the risotto from the heat and stir in half the Parmesan until it melts. Transfer the risotto to warmed bowls. Top with the remaining cheese, garnish with flat-leaf parsley or bay leaves, and serve at once.

SERVES 6

2 tbsp olive oil or vegetable oil

generous 1 cup risotto rice

2 garlic cloves, crushed

1 onion, chopped

2 celery stalks, chopped

1 red or green bell pepper, seeded and chopped

8 oz/225 g button mushrooms, thinly sliced

1 tbsp chopped fresh oregano or 1 tsp dried oregano

4 cups boiling vegetable stock

$1/4$ cup sun-dried tomatoes in olive oil, drained and chopped (optional)

salt and pepper

$1/2$ cup finely grated Parmesan cheese

to garnish

fresh flat-leaf parsley sprigs or bay leaves

Risotto with Artichoke Hearts

Drain the artichoke hearts, reserving the liquid, and cut them into quarters.

Heat the oil with 2 tablespoons of the butter in a deep pan over medium heat until the butter has melted. Stir in the onion and cook gently, stirring occasionally, for 5 minutes, or until soft and starting to turn golden. Do not brown.

Add the rice and mix to coat in oil and butter. Cook, stirring constantly, for 2–3 minutes, or until the grains are translucent. Gradually add the artichoke liquid and the hot stock, a ladle at a time. Stir constantly and add more liquid as the rice absorbs each addition. Increase the heat to medium so that the liquid bubbles. Cook for 15 minutes, then add the artichoke hearts. Cook for an additional 5 minutes, or until all the liquid is absorbed and the rice is creamy. Season to taste.

Remove the risotto from the heat and add the remaining butter. Mix well, then stir in the Parmesan until it melts. Season, if necessary. Spoon the risotto into warmed bowls, garnish with parsley sprigs, and serve at once.

SERVES 4

8 oz/225 g canned artichoke hearts

1 tbsp olive oil

3 tbsp butter

1 small onion, finely chopped

scant $1^1/_2$ cups risotto rice

5 cups boiling vegetable stock

salt and pepper

$^3/_4$ cup freshly grated Parmesan
    or Grana Padano cheese

fresh flat-leaf parsley sprigs,
    to garnish

Vegetarian Paella

Put the saffron threads and water in a small bowl or cup and let infuse for a few minutes.

Meanwhile, heat the oil in a paella pan or wide, shallow skillet and cook the onion over medium heat, stirring, for 2–3 minutes, or until softened. Add the garlic, bell peppers, and eggplant and cook, stirring frequently, for 5 minutes.

Add the rice and cook, stirring constantly, for 1 minute, or until glossy and coated. Pour in the stock and add the tomatoes, saffron and its soaking water, and salt and pepper to taste. Bring to a boil, then reduce the heat and let simmer, shaking the skillet frequently and stirring occasionally, for 15 minutes.

Stir in the mushrooms, green beans, and pinto beans with their can juices. Cook for an additional 10 minutes, then serve immediately.

SERVES 4–6

½ tsp saffron threads

2 tbsp hot water

6 tbsp olive oil

1 Spanish onion, sliced

3 garlic cloves, minced

1 red bell pepper, seeded and sliced

1 orange bell pepper, seeded and sliced

1 large eggplant, cubed

1 cup medium-grain paella rice

2½ cups vegetable stock

1 lb/450 g tomatoes, peeled and chopped

salt and pepper

4 oz/115 g button mushrooms, sliced

4 oz/115 g green beans, halved

14 oz/400 g canned pinto beans

Flamenco Eggs

Preheat the oven to 350°F/180°C. Heat the olive oil in a large, heavy-bottom skillet. Add the onion and garlic and cook over low heat, stirring occasionally, for 5 minutes, or until softened. Add the red bell peppers and cook, stirring occasionally, for an additional 10 minutes. Stir in the tomatoes and parsley, season to taste with salt and cayenne and cook for an additional 5 minutes. Stir in the corn kernels and remove the skillet from the heat.

Divide the mixture among 4 individual ovenproof dishes. Make a hollow in the surface of each using the back of a spoon. Break an egg into each depression.

Bake in the preheated oven for 15–25 minutes, or until the eggs have set. Serve hot.

SERVES 4

4 tbsp olive oil

1 onion, thinly sliced

2 garlic cloves, finely chopped

2 small red bell peppers, seeded and chopped

4 tomatoes, peeled, seeded and chopped

1 tbsp chopped fresh parsley

salt and cayenne pepper

7 oz/200 g canned corn kernels, drained

4 eggs

Egg-Fried Rice with Vegetables

Heat the oil in a wok or large skillet and sauté the garlic and chiles for 2–3 minutes.

Add the mushrooms, snow peas, and corn, and stir-fry for 2–3 minutes before adding the soy sauce, sugar, and basil. Stir in the rice.

Push the mixture to one side of the wok and add the eggs to the bottom. Stir until lightly set before combining into the rice mixture.

If you wish to make the crispy onion topping, heat the oil in another skillet and sauté the onions until crispy and brown. Serve the rice topped with the onions.

SERVES 4

2 tbsp vegetable or peanut oil

2 garlic cloves, finely chopped

2 fresh red chiles, seeded and chopped

4 oz/115 g button mushrooms, sliced

2 oz/55 g snow peas, halved

2 oz/55 g baby corn, halved

3 tbsp Thai soy sauce

1 tbsp light brown sugar

a few Thai basil leaves

3 cups rice, cooked and cooled

2 eggs, beaten

for the crispy onion topping (optional)

2 tbsp vegetable or peanut oil

2 onions, sliced

Spiced Basmati Pilaf

Place the rice in a strainer and wash well under cold running water. Drain. Trim off most of the broccoli stalk and cut into small florets, then quarter the stalk lengthwise and cut diagonally into 1-cm/½-inch pieces.

Heat the oil in a large pan. Add the onions and broccoli stalks and cook over low heat, stirring frequently, for 3 minutes. Add the mushrooms, rice, garlic, and spices and cook for 1 minute, stirring, until the rice is coated in oil.

Add the boiling stock and season to taste with salt and pepper. Stir in the broccoli florets and return the mixture to a boil. Cover, reduce the heat, and cook over low heat for 15 minutes without uncovering the pan.

Remove the pan from the heat and let the pilaf stand for 5 minutes without uncovering. Remove the whole spices, add the raisins and pistachios, and gently fork through to fluff up the grains. Serve the pilaf hot.

SERVES 4

2½ cups basmati rice

6 oz/175 g broccoli, trimmed

6 tbsp vegetable oil

2 large onions, chopped

8 oz/225 g button mushrooms, sliced

2 garlic cloves, crushed

6 cardamom pods, split

6 whole cloves

8 black peppercorns

1 cinnamon stick or piece of cassia bark

1 tsp ground turmeric

5 cups boiling vegetable stock or water

salt and pepper

⅓ cup seedless raisins

½ cup unsalted pistachios, coarsely chopped